Make the Most of Available Personnel with

FOOTBALL'S
MODERN
F·L·E·X·I·N·G
OFFENSE

by Ken Lyons

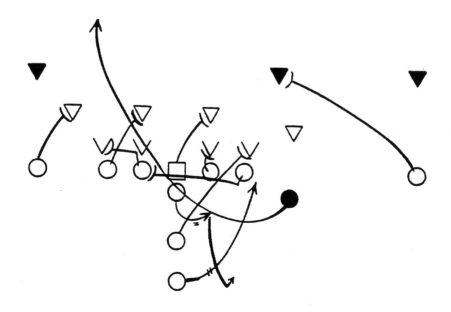

Library of Congress Cataloging-in-Publication Data

Lyons, Ken, 1936-

Make the Most of Available Personnel with Football's
 Modern Flexing Offense/Ken Lyons

Library of Congress Card Number: 00-193119

ISBN: 0970595212

Printed in the United States of America

SHAUGHNESSY PRINTING COMPANY
220 Caillavet Street
Biloxi, Mississippi 39530

Cover Photo by Courtesy of the University of Southern Mississippi

THE IDEAL QUEST:

1) To **Redeem** (our soul)
2) To **Assist** (others)
3) To **Enhance** (family/friendships)
4) To **Strive** (individually)
5) To **Imprint** (society)

DEDICATION

I once again dedicate my second and third books on offensive football to my mother and father, the late Mamie and Louis T. Lyons, who gave me the loving guidance, encouragement, patience, and a balance of values within a stable home environment during the formative, developmental years of my youth. I express my gratitude, as well, to my faithful brothers Jerry and the late Louis Lyons, who gave their backing at critical times when I needed it the most.

I wish to include my four outstanding sons, David, Brent, Jeff, and Michael for the happiness and proud moments they bring into my life--and for their help during the development of this manuscript.

ACKNOWLEDGMENT

I wish to express my sincerest appreciation to Bess Martin, and to Will and Maggie Clingon, for their critique during the early stages of this complex project, and to Susan Kolwicz of Prentice Hall, Inc., for her professional advice and guidance.

My sincerest gratitude is extended to my mentors from the Gulfport (Ms) City School System, Coaches (1) Bert Jenkins, who gave me a start into the coaching field, (2) W. H. "Buddy" Watkins, Frank Young, Edwin H. Roberts, and H.D. Wells, who guided me through the fundamental applications of the game, (3) Lindy Callahan, who influenced me with his organizational and leadership skills, (4) Roland Dale, both at Gulfport High and the University of Southern Mississippi, who provided the professional inspiration and direction, and to (5) Thad "Pie" Vann, and Clyde "Heifer" Stewart of the University of Southern Mississippi, who provided a solid foundation of college-level tutoring. To all my mentors, I wish to thank each of them for teaching me the values of dependability, loyality, pride, and perseverance in career and everyday-life endeavors.

I wish to thank, also, my associate coach and friend, Larry Ramsey, for his input and support.

Ken Lyons

CONTENTS

INTRODUCTION

At last--a portrayal of offensive football that culminates a true end-product evolution of established offensive attacks. This integrated offensive system retains the credibility of all backfield members as true contributors to its running and passing schemes, alike. This presentation, in part, will include...

A) *A modern offensive concept--a "flexing offense"--that conveys the ways and means to field a basic, yet complete and potent, run/pass attack!* The play series designed for the flexing offense is highly efficient, and serves as an excellent guide for coaches who seek to sort out the overwhelming influx of innovations that are put into use by collegiate and professional football teams. The concept of the flexing offense is an extension of a Slot-I offensive attack, which is carefully planned and illustrated in detail, and can be expanded easily into a multiple offensive system (below).

B) *A simplified means of deploying multiple formations, through a structured "Multiflex" offense!* The Multiflex plan places its emphasis upon the usage of varied formations without bringing about player confusion and/or mistakes. The Multiflex plan of attack, which is explained and illustrated, features a consistent play format with a *stable set of assignments for all positions.*

C) *A coverage of useful organizational designs and philosophies!* Efficient organization that is guided by an understanding of the complexities of the problem areas is "the real key" to a coach's successful management and operation of his program.

I hope that you will find this information easy to read and enjoyable, as well as informative and gratifying. Although the Flexing Offense is a culmination of the author's professional quest, the focus is on a *REVELATION* and not upon any individual.

Ken Lyons

I

F L E X I N G THE I-FORMATION

As a starting point for this football guidebook, the author will be presenting his version of an elite offensive system that has emerged from an enduring evolution of run/pass football. This offensive system--an "end product" of its surviving forerunners--could be referred to, generally, as a **Flexing** Offense. The principles of this "flexing offense" can be used to alter or transform football's dominant plays to a better advantage by improving the efficiency of it's personnel. Although no single alignment or system can guarantee magical success, the process of flexing should help improve the application of blocking technique for all linemen and the slot back. The fullback also can become a part of the flexing process by aligning in a position behind one of the guard-tackle B-gaps, rather than directly behind the center. As a fringe benefit, furthermore, the tight end and slot back in a flexed alignment should experience congestion-free releases from the scrimmage line when blocking up the field, or when running pass routes. As with any principle of offense, however, flexing will work to its best advantage, as might be expected, when <u>applied with purpose.</u>

An alignment flex, in itself, will aid in equalizing a weight disparity against opponents who have a physical advantage, providing the smaller athletes can gain an "edge" in quick-strike capability. This "equalizing factor" can help boost individual confidence, and, indirectly, fortify the overall confidence of the entire team. By flexing the alignment of a basic Slot-I formation into Flex-I hybrids, a <u>systematic way both to loosen a defense</u> and/or <u>gain desirable blocking angles</u> upon defensive personnel can be achieved. This is especially important, to reiterate, when attempting to compete with athletes who are lean in physique or lacking in experience, maturity, or talent. The accordion process of tightening and spreading the horizontal alignments of the scrimmage-line blockers should be equally helpful to gifted and non gifted athletes, alike.

The concept of flexing is partly contingent, however, upon a use of the <u>passing attack</u> as an <u>inclusive part</u> of its basic attack--since this will usually soften the coverage of linebackers and defensive backs. The tangible ingredients necessary to generate a productive attack, however, can not depend upon a lone process. The overall format of the running plays and pass patterns should be resourceful and harmonious within itself. Simplicity in the structure of communication, terminology, and method of application also is vital to the success of a consistent winner. To be truly effective, though, one should address the reality that <u>good team morale</u> usually will determine the eventual success of any process, system, or team effort--tending to the morale of both the individual player and to the team as a collective group, therefore, should be priority.

From a career-long quest, in an idealistic search for the ultimate, a flexible system is hereby presented with the hope that it will reveal new insights to all involved coaches and fans, alike. Herein the reader will find an offensive zenith, of sorts, that portrays modern football at its best.

The Flex-I

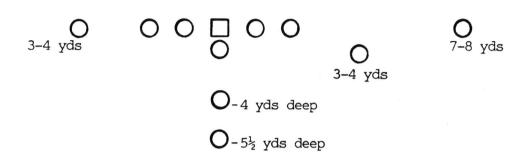

The alignment concept of the Flex-I represents a compromise between a standard Slot-I (tight end opposite the slot back) and a Pro Spread-I. With the tight end and slot back both aligned in a three-to-four yard "flexed" position, inside blocking angles (leverages) are improved and receiver releases are usually free from defensive congestion. This flexed-receiver alignment tends to loosen the defensive perimeter, therefore it is very conducive to option plays as a part of its running attack.

> There are two reasons for flexing a Slot-I formation. Whichever works to the best advantage, the flexing variations should either compress the opposing defense inward or expand it outward, as necessary. A primary consideration of the flexed receivers should be to gain an advantageous blocking angle or one-on-one blocking position on the critical play-side assignments.

> The standard line splits for the guards are two feet from the center, and the tackles split three feet from their guards. Within the concept of flexing, however, both guards and tackles should adjust their line splits whenever their angles can be improved within a certain blocking scheme, such as trap blocking, in example. The offensive line, ideally speaking, should widen their splits on inside runs, and then tighten their line splits on wide runs--or whenever the interior gaps need to be secured against an anticipated onslaught of defensive blitzing. The philosophical concept of flexing is to explore the "game of inches and leverages" to the best advantage of each offensive lineman and receiver!

> When the tight end and slot back are aligned in a flexed position, a "working distance" split of 3 to 4 yards should be taken from their offensive tackles. This 3-4 yard flexed spacing will give the flexed end and slot back the free space, as stated earlier, to block inside and to release from the line on a pass route. The opposing defense, thereby, will usually soften the pass coverage and running-game containment of its corner backs against a flex, but "bump and run" tactics should be expected when the defense is about to use a linebacker blitz.

THE OFFSET FLEX-I

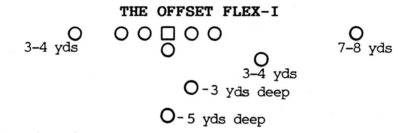

The alignment concept of the Offset Flex-I is the same as that of the tandem-backfield Flex-I. The blocking leverage for the fullback is improved somewhat to the offset side either when blocking a linebacker, a defensive end or the secondary's run-support defender, which is the supporting outside linebacker or strong safety at the split end side, and the corner back at the flexed/tight end side.

> The usual offset guideline for the fullback is to align either behind the designated offensive guard or to the rear of the guard-tackle gap. In the latter case, the fullback may opt to align closer to the line. An offset alignment may give the fullback a different perspective in his three-way role of a blocker, runner, and receiver, which is due to his changed angle of approach into the scrimmage line.

> The offset alignment of the fullback alters the bilateral balance of the running-play format into a distinct direct-side/counter-side format. A predictability in play-calling tendencies can be somewhat avoided to either side of the line, however, by sending the fullback into "flash" motion. Flash motion is run horizontally from a quick burst of speed, using three steps to the formation's weak side, which serves the purpose of redirecting the running and passing strength in the backfield.

Flash Motion to Flexed End Side

> Flash motion is used primarily to (A) DISRUPT defensive recognition, (B) ADJUST the strength of the formation to counter defensive tactics that may be taken to restrict a favored part of the offensive attack, and (C) EXPLOIT areas of vulnerability in the opposition's defensive alignment.

Applying Vertical-Flex Principles

It is highly recommended that the guards and tackles refrain from "crowding" the line-of-scrimmage when in formation, as once practiced by teams of past generations. Short-yardage plays may be an exception, at times, because there are situations where a one-step distance from the opposition can be advantageous with quick-striking plays, using one-on-one blocking. Since a majority of present-day offensive systems appear to rely upon blocking patterns, however, a BACK-SET (vertical flex) alignment adjustment taken behind the line of scrimmage has gained popular appeal. This back-set level will *enhance angle-blocking principles for a majority of blocking schemes for the linemen.*

| The back-set adjustment of the linemen's vertical-flex alignment can give the following advantages:

(1) Play side blockers can have better control of their opponent's slant, loop, and stunt charges because the reaction distance and reflex time for each blocker is lengthened to his advantage.

(2) Down-blocking techniques to the blocker's inside can be focused on gap zones, instead of specific defenders who may, at times, prove to be superior in agility and mobility, alike.

(3) Pulling and trapping angles for the guards and tackles are improved tremendously.

(4) Interference from defensive linemen can be *eliminated* from the back-set, vertical flex stances of the offensive linemen when using on side blocking schemes that involve angle, cross, and trap blocking.

(5) The back side guard and tackle also can execute their cut-off blocking schemes in their inside gaps without interference from a defensive linemen, when using a back-set alignment. Such schemes include scoop blocking, and a similar "Play Side Track" combination block between the back side guard and center, and the "Down Lineman Zone" blocking guideline for the back side tackle (refer to forthcoming Running Play diagrams in this chapter).

Appreciation and acknowledgment is extended to the author's friend and former line coach, Millard Roberson, for his inspiration and input into the formulation of the vertical-flex concept that is designed to improve blocking-scheme efficiency.

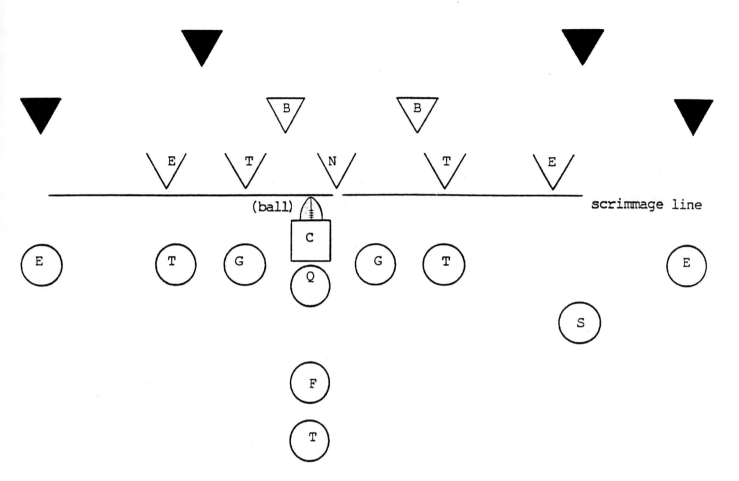

ILLUSTRATION OF LINEMEN'S
BACK-SET ALIGNMENT FROM
THE SCRIMMAGE LINE (ball).
Note that the alignment of
the back-set stances does
not enhance a quick-strike
capability--but it <u>does improve angle, combination,
and gap-control blocking</u>
advantages for the linemen,
while curtailing disruption
tactics from the defense.

A PLAY NOMENCLATURE

(left side)	(play name)	(right side)
"LEFT"	WHAM	"RIGHT"
"LEFT"	COUNTER WHAM	"RIGHT"
7	SWEEP	8
"LEFT"	BOOTLEG	"RIGHT"
21	TACKLE TRAP	22
3	SPIKE	4
3	SPIKE OPTION	4
5	SLANT	6
27	COUNTER REVERSE	28
-	*GOOSE (WEDGE)	-

	(patterns)	
3 Spike	QUICK PASS	4 Spike
13 Pass	MISDIRECTION	14 Pass
"LEFT"	WAGGLE PASS	"RIGHT"
13 Pass	WHEEL	14 Pass
13 Pass	'X'	14 Pass
13 Pass	SHOVEL	14 Pass
13 Pass	SCREEN RIGHT/LEFT	14 Pass
17 Pass	DIVIDE	18 Pass
17 Pass	SPLIT	18 Pass

Clarifying Comment: In the above nomenclature, the only two player positions that have designated numbers are the quarterback (who is #1) and the slot back (who is #2). The fullback and tailback do not have assigned numbers--each athlete is specialized to run certain plays. The majority of running plays will designate the hole number to be hit and the type of play that is run (in example, "3 Spike," which hits over left guard. The Spike Option does not change to an outside number, however, because it is an extension of the Spike play). Special blocking schemes, such as the Wham and Screen Pass, in example, are specified by their left or right direction--not by a designated hole number. *The Goose (Wedge) play, which is a short-yardage "quarterback sneak" up the middle, is described in the coverage of the Spike play and also within Chapter V (Multiflex Merger).

An Overview of I-Backfield Advantages

*When the fullback and tailback are aligned in a tandem, a major part of the running attack will be balanced. This depends, however, upon the alignment of the opposing defense, since it's a game of numbers-and-position. From a tandem, the fullback usually fulfills a role of lead blocker, which gives an aspect of power to the offense equally to both sides of the line. He provides deception by providing false "read-keys" to the defense when misdirection plays are run by the tailback or slot back, since the fullback always goes opposite the play's counter-flow.

*The most dependable and gifted ball carrier on the squad can be designated to run with the football a majority of the time, which is definitely a plus factor.

*The centralized alignment of the tailback enhances his usage of peripheral vision in seeing "daylight" openings in the scrimmage line, thus enhancing his perceptual ability to "run with authority" at the point of attack.

*A specialized blocker can be designated to fulfill the rugged blocking role of the fullback. If the Offset alignment is featured, however, a fullback with less blocking prowess can perform adequately due to the change in blocking leverage to the Offset side. An Offset fullback can contribute significantly as a "hidden" pass receiver, also, when he approaches the battle zone as a would-be blocker and slips through the line on a pass route.

*The slot back can be a small athlete in size. He can be specialized effectively, however, for his combined talents, first as a receiver and a reliable blocker, and, secondly, for his finesse as a misdirection-play ball carrier.

Other I-Formation Advantages

*An I-backfield alignment is generally acknowledged for its power-blocking potential and capability of providing a solid goal line-to-goal line attack.

*I-formation systems that align in a true fullback/tailback tandem have an advantage of using a mirrored attack, both to the left and right sides of the opposition's defensive front.

*The tandem and offset alignments of an I-backfield have favorable fullback/tailback blocking positions. When protecting the quarterback on pull-up and roll-out passes, the fullback is usually assigned to block the defensive end and the tailback is usually assigned to control/block a blitzing linebacker.

*The slot back can and should be used as a fourth running back for misdirection plays. He should seldom be removed from the proximity of the backfield, therefore, for an extended time.

PERSONNEL QUALIFICATIONS (Coach's Wish List)

QUARTERBACK

(1) An accurate, cool-headed passer should be considered first, then running skills considered second. If the top quarterback candidate happens to be a gifted option-play runner, but a less-gifted passer, however, then adapt to his abilities by running option plays more often and throwing less often, with related play-action passes emphasized.

(2) Leadership qualities must be a strong priority in selecting the best candidate. This includes on-and-off the field behavior in regards to loyality to team and coaching staff, and to his adherence to team rules. Quiet leaders can be as effective as the outspoken.

(3) Football intelligence and "coachability" are big pluses in making the top-choice selection between various quarterback candidates (the winner must demonstrate and prove his ability to "move the offense" up the field in live-scrimmage situations).

(4) Mechanical coordination is imperative for running and passing plays, alike! As a passer, the quarterback must attain the skill level to complete his timed pass releases with the timed route/pattern breaks of his receivers,. This process demands dedication patience, and persistence, with extra time spent on the field to fine-tune the timing.

(5) A clear, strong, and commanding voice is an important asset. To some extend, however, voice control is projected through self confidence, so develop quarterback self assuredness through controlled repetitions and rehearsals during drill sessions.

TAILBACK

(1) Most productive runner on squad! Must be adept at "running for daylight." Must have capability to find and pursue the "soft spots" in the defensive front.

(2) Required to carry ball always in outside arm to protect it with body when struck by tacklers.

(3) An unselfish attitude is a position demand! Although the majority of play-call carries are predetermined in the tailback's favor, he cannot be the one to keep count. The loyalty of squad-member must be __nutured__! Everyone must feel that they are an appreciated contributor and a part of the overall team success.

(4) Must be durable as a runner. Conditioning will develop stamina and toughness.

(5) Speed is important because it brings "good luck." When breaking through the scrimmage line, an explosive excelleration is the best luck!

FULLBACK

(1) A powerful inside runner and a strong, dependable blocker is the mandate for this position.

(2) If fullback is physically small, he must be lightning-quick and clever as a blocker.

(3) Should be reliable as a ball carrier for the important Spike play. Must protect ball with arms and hands through battle zone, and be forceful enough to break through congestion in the line.

SLOT BACK

(1) Must be quick and agile as a receiver and runner.

(2) Must be a sure-handed receiver, second only to split end. Physical height is not important, since a majority of his route receptions are from an inside-to-outside angle.

(3) Clever running instincts on misdirection plays are invaluable at this position.

(4) Must be a hard-nosed and intelligent blocker. Flexed spacing can help to equalize a disparity in size when blocking a defensive end or the corner support (outside linebacker or strong safety).

SPLIT END

(1) Must be athletically rangy in running, jumping, and catching the football in a crowd of defenders. Pass receptions often will be made from an inside vantage point.

(2) Must be reliable as a Force Blocker upon his covering defender.

(3) Should have the adeptness to comprehend the secondary coverages of the opposing defense and exercise his capability and initiative to capitalize at opportune moments.

(4) Sure-handed pass receiving skills are an absolute essential!

FLEXED END/TIGHT END

(1) Must be a cunning blocker when actuating Flexed Spacing, but physical enough also to align as a tight end and execute Inside, Load, and Reach Blocking assignments.

(2) Should have fair-to-good pass receiving hands.

(3) Should have average running speed , at least (no elephants).

TACKLES

(1) The quickest linemen are to be assigned here (must block linebackers).

(2) Must be a dependable Trap Blocker (quick feet are a necessity).

(3) Hustle is vital to cut off linebackers, for pass protection (to block the back side defensive end), and to Rake-and-Release Block to second level (linebacker zone) from the back side of a play. "LAZY FEET" CANNOT PLAY AT THIS POSITION!

GUARDS

(1) Heavier linemen to be assigned here (must control middle gaps to prevent leakage).

(2) Dependable performers are needed for one-on-one blocking (Area Rule), to Reach Block, and to Scoop Block the inside gap from the back side of a play.

(3) Required to stay mentally alert to communicate "Gap Call" blocking situations to his affiliate linemen and slot back.

CENTER

(1) To decide the starting position for center, the first consideration should go to the player who can snap the ball accurately and consistently to the quarterback, who is dependable from play to play, and also reliable in varying down-and-distance situations!

(2) Linemen with physical size should be screened, also, but their feet typically should be quicker than those of the guards, because the center does not have the advantage of back-setting into a vertical flex, behind the ball, as savored by the guards and tackles.

(3) The center may be asked to control the on side A-gap without help, at times, when confronting a defensive front that could tie-up the guards with an unusual gap-control alignment. This is where the importance of size and foot quickness becomes obvious.

(4) The center will be required, oftentimes, to Fill Block into the back side A-gap for the purpose of sealing the vacated area left by a pulling guard.

★　　★　　★　　★　　★　　★　　★

With the personnel qualification now behind us, we shall now proceed with the play agenda, concepts, and illustrations that relate to the F L E X I N G   O F F E N S E.

RUNNING PLAYS

(1) The **Wham** is perhaps the most consistent and reliable play in football! The traditional version of the **Wham** play includes a companion quarterback **Keep**, and also an **Option Keep-or-Pitch** to the slot back in motion. The latter can be categorized as a combination tailback belly and quarterback belly-option play, due to the quarterback's footwork mechanics and techniques.

•   The updated version of the **Wham** is, primarily, a tailback Lead-Draw play. The backfield mechanics of the lead-draw version has the initial appearance of an oncoming Pull-Up (pocket) or Roll-Out Pass, with the hint of a possible hand-off to the tailback. This built-in lead-draw threat helps to slow the play recognition of the defense. The main benefit of the lead-draw concept, therefore, is that the opposing linebackers first must play with caution in responding either to a pass or run--and the quarterback also can execute the ball exchange to the tailback a step deeper in the backfield. If the defense should linger a moment longer in it's play recognition, the time lapse could make a subtle difference in the success of the play. In the lead-draw version, the tailback usually has a little more time to perceive the blocking position of ALL up-front blockers, not just his lead-blocking fullback.

•   In either play version, however, the tailback must rely and depend upon the fullback as his key blocker! A solid block upon the isolated linebacker, at the point of attack, is essential to the success of the **Wham**. If the isolated linebacker can be stalemated, at best, the tailback has a great opportunity make a clean break into the secondary.

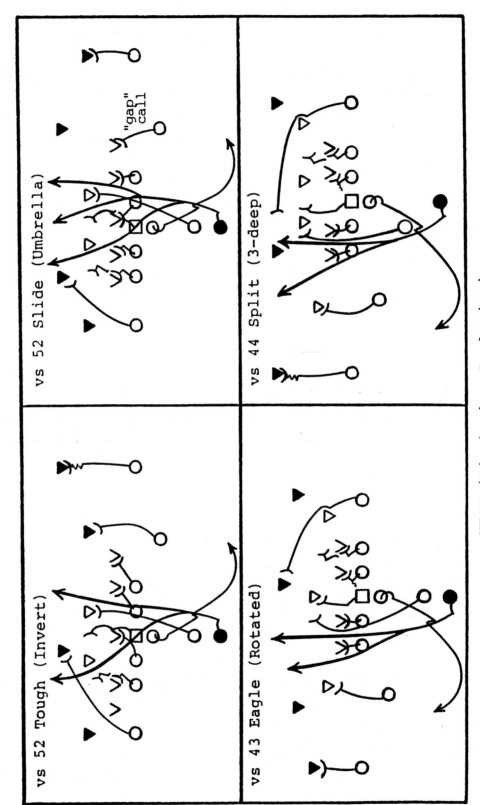

vs 52 Slide (Umbrella)

"gap" call

vs 44 Split (3-deep)

vs 52 Tough (Invert)

vs 43 Eagle (Rotated)

WHAM (Linebacker Isolation)

Play Name: WHAM
<with Keeper alternative>

ASSIGNMENTS & TECHNIQUES + PERSONNEL REQUIREMENTS & STRATEGY

QB- Use the Pivot Step Method: Exit from center with "reverse pivot" footwork. The initial pivot should take place with the on side foot, making a basic 190 degree turn while the back side foot lifts off the ground and simultaneously sways around to the rear with enough force to give impetus to the half turn. As the back side foot is planted, the on side foot follows to the rear while both feet become somewhat parallel to themselves. The momentum of this movement is then transferred to a straight-line run to the exchange zone behind the play side guard at an approximate depth of three-to-four yards. After completing the ball exchange, either set up behind the on side guard or fake/carry-out a **Keeper** around end.

TB- Take a lateral step to the play side with the on side foot and follow alongside with an inside-and-up step with the back side foot. Next, take a direct step with the on side foot directly ahead and receive the football from the quarterback while on the run, about four yards deep in the backfield. Follow the fullback to the "linebacker bubble," and break off his Lead Block! If congestion in the attack area should occur, visually scan for a "soft spot" elsewhere along the line.

FB- Lead Block directly into the inside linebacker at the play side. When facing an even-man front, such as a 4-4-3 or 6-1-4 defense, go through the B-gap to seal-off the middle/inside linebacker. When facing a 4-3-4 defense, whereas a linebacker is aligned over the tackle on the tight end side, consider that linebacker the "isolation target" and Lead Block/Climb Block into him.

SB- Block the covering outside linebacker or strong safety. Back Side: Secure the C-gap and block in the deep middle. Gap Calls: Block the end man on line (EMOL).

SE- Force Block the corner back--run him up the field as deep as he will go, then "break down" into a semi crouch. Block him nose-to-nose with an uplifting whip of the hands under his shoulder pads, and sustain contact by keeping the feet churning feet. When on back side, run the crease and block in deep middle area.

TE/FLEXED END- Play side: Crack Block into the outside linebacker: if not applicable, block the corner back. If in tight, release outside the defensive end and block the corner back. If a 6-1-4 or a 8-gap defense, block the defensive end. Back Side: Run the back side crease with the intimidation of a developing Crack Block.

PST- Block the #2 defender on the line-of-scrimmage (disregard linebacker).

PSG- Block the #1 defender on the line-of-scrimmage (disregard linebacker).

C- Play Side Track: Cut off gap/linebacker (LB). If a nose guard/defensive lineman (NG/DL) is not present, or if the NG slides toward the BSG when Combo Blocking, release into 2nd level and either block the middle linebacker (MLB) or the back side linebacker (BSLB).

BSG- Down Lineman Zone (DLZ): Block defensive lineman (DL) in the A-gap, over, or back side. Lock up, chop steps, rotate hips inside, and squeeze into inside gap. If Combo Blocking with center, engage NG/BSLB.

BST- Rake and Release (R & R): Rake near forearm under the adjacent shoulder pad of opponent in the B-gap, over, or back side, and then release into 2nd level to block the outside linebacker (OLB).

PERSONNEL CONSIDERATIONS- The tailback should be a clever, durable, and hard-nosed ball carrier who runs with authority and can read his line blocking.

STRATEGY- Use as the #1 play in the offense, on any down-and-distance situation, and in any field zone. To set up an effective play-action passing attack, the **Wham** play should be used extensively!

\<INCLUSION OF A WHAM OPTION IN PLACE OF THE QUARTERBACK KEEPER\>

If an offensive coordinator wishes to use a **Wham Option** play to expand the quarterback play, the following guidelines are offered...

(A)   As a prerequisite, make certain that the quarterback has the dexterity and the mental and physical toughness to run a keep-or-pitch option play. Since the blocking structure of this version of the **Wham Option** accounts for all the down-linemen, the pitch key, by design, is the corner back (corner support defender) on the tight side and the outside linebacker/strong safety on the split end side (a split side option is made possible by the usage of twirl motion by the slot back, as illustrated in the play diagrams). When the quarterback isolates the corner support defender as his option-pitch key, quick pressure from the outside will seldom be experienced during manipulation of the keep-or-pitch phase. This play is, therefore, a low-risk option.

(B)   The quarterback must Pivot Step from center and execute his fake hand off exchange to the tailback with the exact footwork and depth in the backfield as prescribed for the **Wham** play. His feet should be somewhat perpendicular to the scrimmage line when the fake hand off exchange is about to be made to the tailback. His rearfoot should be planted briefly when the tailback is greeted with the extended football, while his inside foot (the one closest to the line of scrimmage) should be brought directly underneath its corresponding shoulder for body balance during the fake exchange. The arm movement of this two-handed ball-exchange fake should be carried out with a brisk arm-ride movement that coincides with the tailback's forward momentum. This arm-ride, although brief, must be sufficient enough to give an impression that the football has been handed off to the tailback. After the tailback clears the arm-ride zone, the quarterback should run a straight-line course "downhill" at the short flank, which generally will be located about a yard outside the defensive end.

(C)   If the defensive alignment on the tight side is a traditional five-man front--with the inside linebacker aligned over the guard--it will be necessary for the tight end to align "in tight" and help block the defensive end in combination with his offensive tackle. This combination block will enable the linemen to retain their wham-blocking scheme and also allow the quarterback to focus on the corner support as the intended pitch key. If a gapped defensive front exists, the tight end, again, must align "in tight" and then down block inside upon the #3 lineman. If the defensive alignment is a balanced, even front, the tight end usually can Flex his position and then Crack Block into the outside linebacker, if aligned to his inside.

·   Since this blocking scheme dictates the play side guard to block the #1 defensive lineman, and the play side tackle to block the #2 defensive lineman, this version of the **Wham Option** will be most effective against even-man fronts and compressed five-man fronts. When this blocking scheme is used against a loose five-man front, the offensive guard and tackle first must block to their outside to tie-up their assigned defensive linemen, then work their feet quickly to "turn" their hips around to an outside-leverage position against their opponents. This procedure must be aided with a staunch **Wham** play fake.

(D)   The slot back should use a 3-step motion technique to attain a desirable pitch relationship 4 yards deep and 4 yards to the outside of his quarterback.

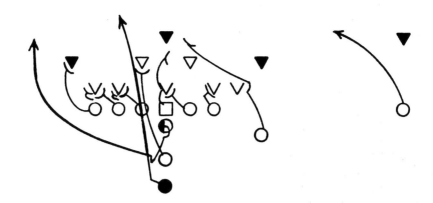

An illustration of the **Wham** play with a quarterback
Keeper innovation as part of a Tailback Belly Series.

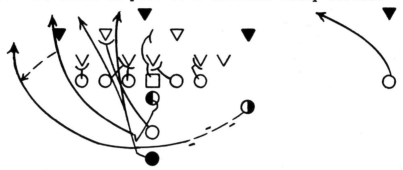

An illustration of an Option Pitch innovation, which is
feasible to the Tight Side when three-step Motion is
used by the slot back to achieve a desirable pitch relationship with the quarterback (4 yards depth and width).

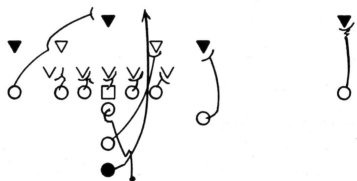

An illustration of the **Wham** play as a part of a Lead-Draw
Series. Since the Keeper and Option plays are NOT a part
of the traditional Lead Draw Series, the opposing defense
may be falsely coaxed into making a false pass-coverage
hesitation or reaction.

Note: An IDEAL WAY to make use of BOTH play methods for
the quarterback is to use the OPTION KEEP-or-PITCH INNO-
VATION when slot back MOTION is utilized, and then make
use of the PULL-UP PASS (Lead Draw) set up when slot back
motion is NOT exercised.

(2) The **Counter Wham** play is perhaps the most potent, yet less complicated, counter play in football. It provides an all-important misdirection play for the tailback, who must have a means to exploit the fast-read reactions of the defense. For the quarterback, it provides an antedote for the hurried responses that the opposing secondary coverages may take in their initial read of the quarterback's roll-out passes. The **Counter Wham** can be identified with the Counter Trey and the somewhat similar Cross Buck plays. <u>The **Counter Wham** play is unique, however, because it uses the back side tackle as the pull-and-lead blocker upon the on side linebacker</u>, who is left isolated at the point-of-attack. In the event of a linebacker blitz, the pulling tackle must be trained to recognize his penetration and, thereby, respond to the situation by trap-blocking him from inside-out.

• As a *fringe benefit*, pulling a tackle from the back side of the line presents absolutely no blocking adjustments in the middle against eight-man defensive fronts, whereas pulling a back side guard often requires enormous blocking adjustments in the middle in order to protect against an impending linebacker blitz or a lineman's gap charge through the middle.

• In the backfield, the quarterback pivot-steps from under the center, rolls-out as if preparing to throw a pass, and then makes a deep hand-off to the tailback. The tailback's footwork and running angles are very important in setting up the misdirection aspect of the play (refer to assignments).

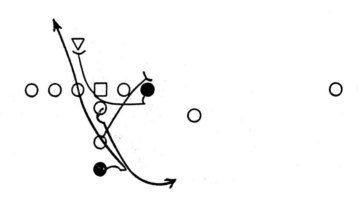

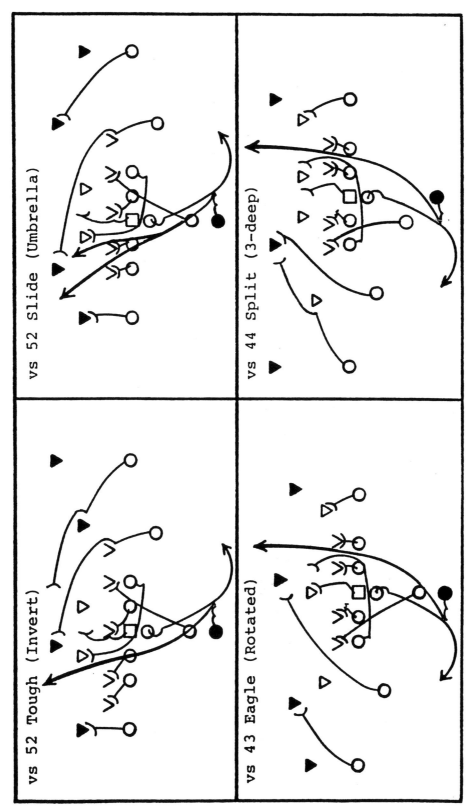

vs 52 Slide (Umbrella)

vs 44 Split (3-deep)

vs 52 Tough (Invert)

vs 43 Eagle (Rotated)

COUNTER WHAM (Linebacker Isolation)

Play Name: COUNTER WHAM

ASSIGNMENTS & TECHNIQUES + PERSONNEL REQUIREMENTS & STRATEGY

QB - Exit from center with a Pivot Step. Then run to the six-yard "fish hook curve" of the roll-out arc-pocket, which rounds-off behind the on side guard. While en route to this area, make a "rear hand-off" to the tailback, about four yards in depth. A rear hand-off means that the quarterback runs in front of the tailback and makes the ball exchange in a backward motion to the waiting arms of the tailback. This ball exchange will take place behind the back side guard, since the tailback is required to take a slide-step in that direction to set up the play's counter effect. After the hand off is made, run the track of the six-yard arc and complete the ritual of a roll-out pass fake.

TB - Take a lateral step to the back side with the on side foot, and follow up with a slide step. Maintain a slight bend in the knees. The quarterback must bring the ball to the tailback for the ball exchange, therefore patience is a necessity when setting up and holding a steady arm-and-stomach pouch for the ball reception (the play side elbow should be held upward). Ample room is available for the counter run, since the quarterback clears in front of the tailback. After the hand off is made, run a deliberate arc for the attack area, locate the back side tackle, and then follow him through the play hole. Read the pulling tackle's blocking position upon the isolated linebacker and then break for daylight from his block.

FB - Step with lead foot, aim at the back side guard's outside foot, and apply an inside-out Climb Block upon the first defender to appear in the B-gap area.

SB - Block the outside linebacker or strong safety (run-support defender). Back Side: Secure the C-gap and block in deep middle. Gap Calls: Block the end man on the line (EMOL).

SE - Force Block the corner back--run him up the field as deep as he will go, then "break down" into a semi crouch. Block him nose-to-nose with an uplifting whip of the hands under his shoulder pads, and sustain contact by keeping the feet churning feet. When on back side, run the crease and block in deep middle area.

TE/FLEXED END - Play side: Crack Block the outside linebacker: if not applicable, block the corner back. If in tight, release outside the defensive end and then block the corner back. If a 6-1-4 or a 8-gap defense, block the #3 opponent. Back side: Run back side crease and block in the deep middle (the near safety)

PST - Block the #2 defender on the line-of-scrimmage (disregard linebacker).

PSG - Block the #1 defender on the line-of-scrimmage (disregard linebacker).

C - Play Side Track: Cut off gap/linebacker (LB). If a nose guard/defensive lineman (NG/DL) is not present, or if the NG slides toward the BSG when Combo Blocking, release into 2nd level and block middle linebacker (MLB) or back side linebacker (BSLB).

BSG - Down Lineman Zone (DLZ): Block defensive lineman (DL) in the A-gap, over, or back side. Lock up, chop steps, rotate hips inside, and squeeze into inside gap. If Combo Blocking with center, engage NG/BSLB.

BST - Pull from line, enter the first opening past the center, and Lead/Climb Block into the isolated, inside linebacker through play side A or B-gap.

PERSONNEL CONSIDERATIONS - The tailback should be a clever, durable and innovative runner with the discipline to follow his lead blocker into the play hole.

STRATEGY - Use after a succession of Pull up or Roll Out passes, or at any time a back side linebacker shows a "fast-flow" response to opposite-side plays.

(3) The **Sweep** play is simplicity personified in its design, both from the Flex-I and Offset Flex-I, and should yield consistent productivity! It is a sound play for any down-and-distance situation. A very favorable blocking scheme for the **Sweep** is the all-purpose G-Pull, whereas the play side guard pulls from the line to his on side flank, usually at the slot side, and proceeds to apply a Kick-Out Block upon the defending strong safety or outside linebacker. During this time, the play side tackle blocks his designated defensive tackle, while the play side slot back applies a Down Block, usually, upon the defensive end. If the tight end is on the play side, he must use a Reach Block to contain the defensive end. If the tight end is aligned in a flex, he should Crack Block into the first linebacker to his inside, which leaves the end man on the line (EMOL) to be blocked by the fullback, or occupied with a Reach Block by the play side tackle.

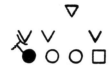

Tight End Reach-Block.

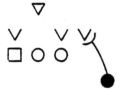

Slot Back Down-Block.

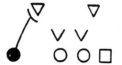

Flexed End Crack Block to inside
w/guard & tackle Reach Blocking.

Other useful blocking Schemes for the Sweep include (1) Reach Blocking, whereas each on side lineman will block any compressed/reduced down lineman who aligns on his outside shoulder, and (2) Numerical Count Blocking, whereas each blocker is directly responsible for an assigned-number defender.

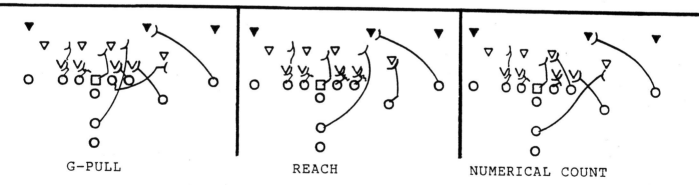

G-PULL   REACH   NUMERICAL COUNT

* The quarterback **Bootleg** is an awesome and natural complement to the **Sweep** and shares the same blocking Scheme. The **Bootleg** can exploit any miscalculations that may occur during the defensive pursuit of the **Sweep** play, in similarity to a wide reverse--especially when the back side defensive end begins to "pinch" to the inside, behind the apparent play flow.

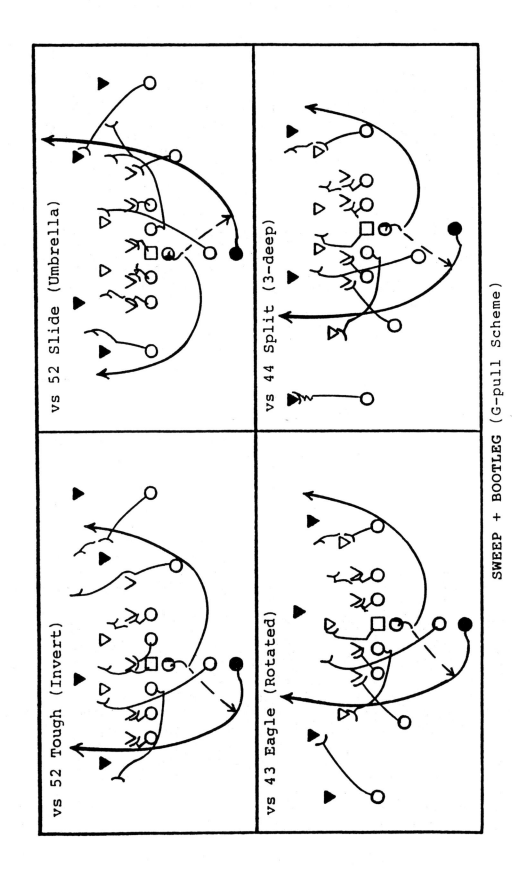

vs 52 Slide (Umbrella)

vs 52 Tough (Invert)

vs 44 Split (3-deep)

vs 43 Eagle (Rotated)

SWEEP + BOOTLEG (G-pull Scheme)

Play Name: SWEEP *(with quarterback Bootleg)*

ASSIGNMENTS & TECHNIQUES + PERSONNEL REQUIREMENTS & STRATEGY

QB- Execute a Pivot Step from center and pitch the football during the spin, at the 5 o'clock position, into the receiving hands of the tailback as he begins his "control run" toward the play side C-gap. Assure that the pitch to the tailback is firm, but soft enough to catch. After pitching the ball, begin to run a three-to-four yard arc in the opposite direction, and then sprint toward the sideline with quick acceleration; on a designated Bootleg, keep the football after faking a pitch to the tailback.

TB- Take a lateral step with the on side foot to the play side, then control-run to the area just outside the C-gap. "Collect" the pitched football with both hands, secure the ball under the outside arm, read the blocking siituation at the "downhill running lane," and break accordingly. The decisions to make are (A) run through the off-tackle C-gap, (B) run through the D-gap, just outside the slot back or tight end, or (C) run through the middle area, after cutting to the back side toward a suspected soft spot, which is usually the linebacker zone.

FB- G-Pull Scheme: Fill Block through the B-gap (aim at inside hip of PST).
    Reach Blocking Scheme: Block pitch support (CB on Tight Side; OLB, or SS on Slot Side).
    Numerical Count Scheme: Block #4 (pitch support). If called toward a flexed-end, block EMOL if unblocked.

SB- G-Pull Scheme: Block the end man on the line (EMOL) aggressively.
    Reach Blocking Scheme: Reach Block the outside opponent (DE/OLB/SS).
    Numerical Count Scheme: Block #3. Back Side: Intimidate #3, then block in the deep middle (free safety).

SE- Block the deep safety (nearest safety in Cover 2; free safety in Cover 3). When on back side, run the crease and block in the deep middle (nearest safety).

TE/FLEXED END- Play side: Block #3; if flexed, Crack Block inside (on Sweep or Bootleg). Back side: Run the back side crease. If flexed, intimidate OLB with a Crack Block along the way into the crease run.

PST- G-Pull Scheme: Block defensive tackle aggressively (outside position).
    Reach Blocking Scheme: Lateral step and Reach Block the covering defender.
    Numerical Count Blocking: Block #2.

PSG- G-Pull Scheme: Pull from line to play side, turn up the field after clearing the EMOL, and then Kick-Out Block the pitch support (CB on the Tight Side; OLB, or SS on the Slot Side).
    Reach Blocking Scheme: Step to outside and Reach block #1 defender. If uncovered, reach step and block in combination with the PST.
    Numerical Count Blocking: Block #1.

C- Play Side Track: Cut off gap/linebacker (LB). If a nose guard/defensive lineman (NG/DL) is not present, or if the NG slides toward the BSG when Combo Blocking, release into 2nd level and either block the middle linebacker (MLB) or the back side linebacker (BSLB).

BSG- Down Lineman Zone (DLZ): Block defensive lineman (DL) in the A-gap, over, or back side. Lock up, chop steps, rotate hips inside, and squeeze into inside gap. If Combo Blocking with center, engage NG/BSLB.

BST- Rake and Release (R & R): Rake near forearm under the adjacent shoulder pad of opponent in the B-gap, over, or back side, and then release into 2nd level to block the outside linebacker (OLB).

PERSONNEL CONSIDERATIONS- A clever, gutsy runner at the tailback position can make the downhill **Sweep** the most powerful inside-outside play in football!

STRATEGY- Use on any down, especially on 1st and 2nd. A great open-field play.

(4) The **Tackle Trap** may be the ultimate trap play in football and could eliminate a need to run other trap designs that could complicate a team's trap-play assignments. When the offensive tackles are designated as the primary pulling linemen in the offensive structure, it is not necessary to alter the internal blocking assignments, and, therefore, the bulky, less-mobile athletes then can be specialized at the guard positions.

The **Tackle Trap** is a devastating misdirection play, especially when used as a "checkmate" to counter the opposition's over-zealous defensive pursuit that often occurs during the running action of the tailback Sweep. The play's greatest attribute, however, is that the opposing linebackers usually experience difficulty in grasping the elusive, against-the-grain running approach that the slot back takes to make his entry into the trap zone from his 3-yard flexed alignment.

The quarterback starts the play with a reverse-spin movement from the center and fakes a pitch-back to the tailback, who, in turn, goes through the motion of running a downhill Sweep. When the spin reaches its 2 o'clock position, make a forward hand-off to the slot back as he makes a frontal pass-by during his trek to the play hole, trailing behind the trap block of his tackle.

The **Misdirection** pass is a beneficial complement to the **Tackle Trap** play by keeping the outside linebacker/strong safety honest (refer to Pass Patterns).

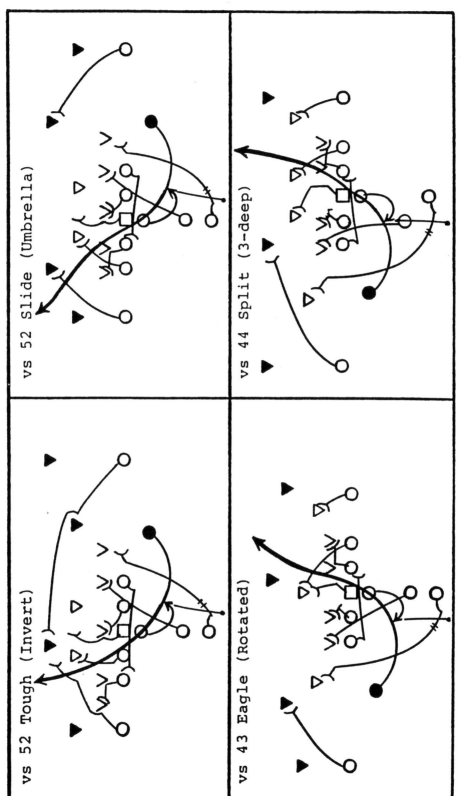

vs 52 Slide (Umbrella)

vs 44 Split (3-deep)

vs 52 Tough (Invert)

vs 43 Eagle (Rotated)

TACKLE TRAP (Middle Trap Scheme)

Play Name: TACKLE TRAP

ASSIGNMENT & TECHNIQUES + PERSONNEL REQUIREMENTS & STRATEGY

QB- Take a Pivot Step from center, fake a pitch with the football to the tailback during the deep spin at the 5 o'clock position and then make an "underneath," forward hand off to the slot back at the 2 o'clock position. After completing the ball exchange, retreat to the pull-up pocket behind the on side guard and simulate the **Misdirection** pass to hold the outside linebacker/strong safety in position.

TB- Take a lateral step with slot side foot, then adjust the follow-up steps to accomodate a controlled run toward the C-gap as a shield blocker. While en route to the C-gap area, coordinate the fake of a two-handed catch with the quarterback's fake ball toss. A convincing fake with the hands can give the defense a false recognition key of an impending sweep, which is invaluable to the success of this play.

FB- Step with lead foot, aim at the back side guard's outside foot and then execute an inside-out Climb Block upon the first defender to appear in the B-gap area.

SB- Take a half-pivoting, backward step at the play's inception to gain depth and also to acquire the timing that is necessary to clear the trap zone just beyond the center. The pathway of approach is somewhat oblong, since the ball exchange is received in front of the quarterback, after he fakes the ball toss.

SE- Run through the corner back/strong safety zone-coverage crease and block in the deep middle.

TE/FLEXED END- Tight alignment; block the end man on line (EMOL). Flexed alignment: Crack Block inside.

PST- Block the inside/middle linebacker; if the linebacker is identified as the PSG's assigned #1 defender, however, then Exit Block outside to leave the covering "trap target" in isolation for the Trap Block. If facing a gapped defensive front that does not have an inside linebacker, Exit Block to the outside defender. Note that the PSG also should Exit Block versus a gapped defense and pick up the B-gap opponent.

PSG- Block the #1 defender; if the "trap target" is the #1 defender, then Exit Block to the outside. If the trap target should be covering the PSG, first execute a forearm "rake" technique under the opponent's outside shoulder pad before stepping outside to initiate the Exit Block. The rake technique will help to widen the trap target and thereby delay his play recognition, which should set him up for the trap block.

C- Play Side Track: Cut off gap/linebacker (LB). If a nose guard/defensive lineman (NG/DL) is not present, or if the NG slides toward the BSG when Combo Blocking, release into 2nd level and block the middle linebacker (MLB) or back side linebacker (BSLB).

BSG- Down Lineman Zone (DLZ): Block defensive lineman (DL) in the A-gap, over, or back side. Lock up, chop steps, rotate hips inside, and squeeze into inside gap. If Combo Blocking with center, engage NG/BSLB.

BST- Pull from line of scrimmage and Trap Block the first penetration to appear beyond the center.

PERSONNEL CONSIDERATIONS- The slot back should have the necessary savvy and quickness to run his track properly through the trap zone, and also possess the "hungry instinct" to capitalize upon the across-the-grain scoring opportunity.

STRATEGY- Use to exploit a zealous linebacker pursuit of the **Sweep** play.

(5) The fullback **Spike** play strikes at the very heart of the defense--in the middle. Since the running drive of the fullback is aimed at the inside leg of his play side guard, he has the leverage to break either into the center-guard gap or into the guard-tackle gap. His quick strike into the line hits at the approximate moment that his blocking linemen are making contact with the defense. This abrupt surge may catch the opposition unsettled, when it follows a series of tailback running plays, especially when used with a quick snap count. The quarterback, after receiving the football exchange from center, should execute a reverse-pivot spin at a depth of one yard and hand the ball to the fullback with a quick-jab motion.

● **Wedge Blocking** can be included easily for the fullback **Spike** play. Each offensive lineman must pinch inside during the snap of the football, interlock shoulder pads with the blocker in advance and thereby form a massive, moving wedge of blockers. The center is usually the apex blocker--when uncovered, the play side guard should become the designated apex. When the defenders are raised upward by the blocking surge, and their traction is lost, a touchdown for the fullback can be the end result. The slot back should either arc inside to protect the C-gap or down-block directly to his inside to tie up the defensive end by aiming his headgear in front of his target to stifle his charge and prevent penetration into the backfield.

In the diagram below, the **Fullback Wedge** play is illustrated with a cross-buck fake, which complements the **Counter Reverse** play. This backfield action is inherently compatible with the **Quick Pass**, with the quarterback releasing the football after his jab fake to the fullback (also illustrated).

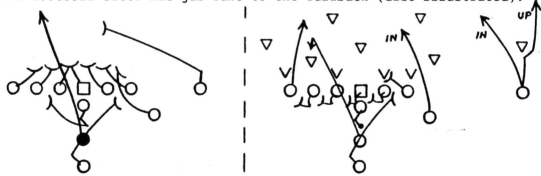

* In regard to Wedge Blocking, this blocking scheme can be applied with maximum efficiency when used in combination with a silent-count "quarterback sneak" **Goose** play. The fullback should be assigned to block the end man on the line at the tight side from an inside-out angle and the tailback should be assigned to seal-off the slot side C-gap, as a security blocker, from an inside-out angle (see illustration below).

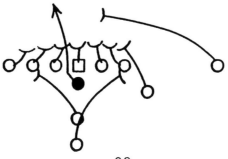

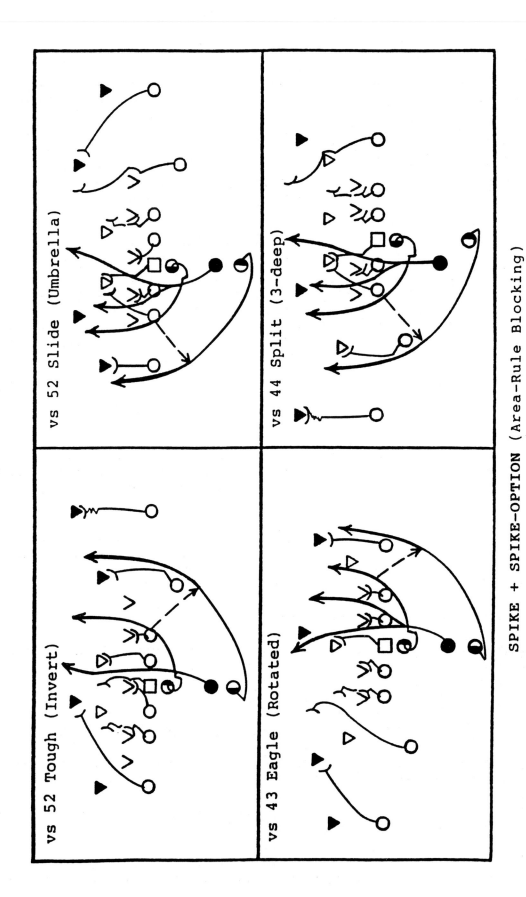

vs 52 Tough (Invert)

vs 52 Slide (Umbrella)

vs 43 Eagle (Rotated)

vs 44 Split (3-deep)

SPIKE + SPIKE-OPTION (Area-Rule Blocking)

-30-

Play Name: SPIKE

ASSIGNMENTS & TECHNIQUES + PERSONNEL REQUIREMENTS & STRATEGY

QB- Pivot-step from center and execute hand off to the fullback directly behind the center at an approximate depth of one yard. At the completion of the pivot, a momentary freeze should take place with the shoulders in a perpendicular plane to the scrimmage line. The feet should be near-parallel and about a foot apart as the fullback makes his approach to the hand-off zone during his drive for his "landmark" behind the play side guard. The football should be handed-off to the fullback with a quick jab motion, using both hands for maximum security. As the fullback clears, he should run a straight track for the inside shoulder of the end man on the line, and then simulate an option-pitch to the wide-arcing tailback. On occasion, a fake Quick-Pass can be simulated, as well, instead of an option-play fake, which helps to delay the response of the inside linebacker.

TB- Begin with a counter-step to distract the play-flow key of the linebackers and to improve the blocking positioning of the offensive linemen, then run an option-pitch course to maintain a pitch-relationship distance of four yards in depth from the quarterback and four yards to his outside.

FB- Explode from stance, taking the first step with the on side foot. Keep the shoulders low and drive forward with a low center of gravity to accept the hand-off with inside elbow upward. Arms must be kept open and parallel with the top hand hanging downward and the bottom hand facing upward. Keep ball covered with both arms as the entry is made into the line. Strike forcefully and with authority, breaking off the block of the play side guard, and then slice into the open alley-way. The "instinct" to read the blocking and then slice into a line opening must be developed through successful repetitions in training drills.

SB- Block the pitch support (outside linebacker or strong safety) who provides support coverage for the end man on the line (EMOL). Back Side: Secure the C-gap and block in deep middle. Gap Call: Block the EMOL.

SE- Force Block the corner back (run him up the field as deep as he will go, then "break-down" into a semi crouch, block him nose-to-nose with an uplifting whip of the hands under his shoulder pads, and keep feet churning to sustain contact). When on the back side, run through the corner back/free safety coverage crease and block in deep middle.

TE/FLEXED END- Play side: Block the pitch support (either the outside linebacker or corner back). Back side: Run the back side corner back/free safety coverage crease with the intimidation of a linebacker Crack Block.

PST- Block the #two defender from the center (lineman or linebacker).

PSG- Block the #one defender from the center (lineman or linebacker).

C- Play Side Track: Cut off gap/linebacker (LB). If a nose guard/defensive lineman (NG/DL) is not present, or if the NG slides toward the BSG when Combo Blocking, release to 2nd level and block middle linebacker (MLB) or back side linebacker (BSLB).

BSG- Down Lineman Zone (DLZ): Block defensive lineman (DL) in the A-gap, over, or back side. Lock up, chop steps, rotate hips inside, and squeeze into inside gap. If Combo Blocking with center, engage NG/BSLB.

BST- Rake and Release (R & R): Rake near forearm under the adjacent shoulder pad of opponent in the B-gap, over, or back side, and then release into 2nd level to block the outside linebacker (OLB).

PERSONNEL CONSIDERATIONS- The fullback should be a quick, rugged runner with strong legs and have the capability to "break" off the blocking of his on side guard.

STRATEGY- Use as a change-up play to attack the very heart of the defense. It is a good 2nd down play, especially after using the option. The Spike play helps to set up usage of the Quick Pass at strategic moments.

The **Spike**, **Spike Option,** and **Quick Pass** can be blended into a self-sustaining series of its own due to the likeness of the quarterback's footwork and hand-off mechanics. This trio should work in unison as a dynamic complement to the remaining plays in the Flexing Offense.

*   The fullback **Spike** can be altered into a **Roll** play to function as a built-in counter play for the downhill **Sweep.** In the design of the **Roll,** the fullback takes a quick lateral step to the on side before "rolling" behind the block of his play side guard. At this time, he can either drive into the B-gap, or cut-back inside against the pursuit of the defense. This footwork action of the fullback, therefore, gives the **Roll** play certain counter-strike advantages. The premise of the play, however, is that the presence of a quick-striking, yet flexible fullback is necessary and needed in every I-formation offense--and the **ROLL** play, thereby, can supply an option-free offensive system with a hard-nosed demeanor that is a part of the **Sweep/Bootleg** series.

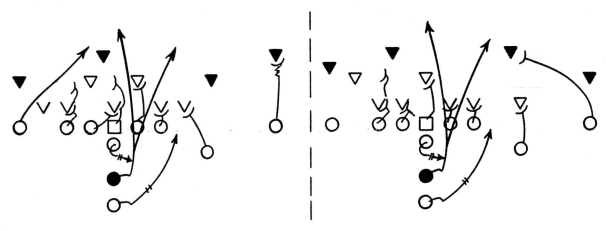

An illustrated Counter Effect of the **Roll** Play When Utilized as Part of the Sweep Series. The Blocking Rules that apply are Identical to Those of the **Spike** play.

Play Name: ROLL

<an alternative fullback Dive play from the Sweep series>

ASSIGNMENTS & TECHNIQUES + PERSONNEL REQUIREMENTS & STRATEGY

QB- Execute a Pivot Step from center, fake a two-handed ball toss to the tailback at the 5 o'clock position—to simulate a downhill toss **Sweep**—and then make a jab-motion hand off to the fullback, at the 3 o'clock position.

TB- Take a lateral step with on side foot, then adjust the follow-up steps to accommodate a controlled run toward the C-gap as a shield blocker. While en route to the C-gap area, coordinate the fake of a two-handed catch with the quarterback's fake ball toss. A convincing fake with the hands can give the defense a false recognition key of an impending sweep, which is invaluable to the success of this play.

FB- Take a lateral step with play side foot, to gain both the needed width and the necessary delay for timing. The second step, and the successive steps thereafter, should point directly ahead, behind the play side guard. Concentrate on running a consistent track toward the play side guard, his land mark, to insure an error-free ball exchange. The ball should be received from the quarterback with the inside forearm held upward, then secured under the outside arm. Read the blocking up front to determine the best cut to make into the line, either inside or outside. The line openings usually will occur between the boundaries of the play side B-gap and the back side A-gap, which gives the **Roll** an advantage similar to a counter-play.

SB- Block the #3 defender from the A-gap. Back Side: Secure the C-gap and block in the deep middle. Gap Call: Block the end man on the line (EMOL).

SE- Play Side: Sprint toward and block the near safety versus a 4-deep, and use Force Blocking tactics against a corner back versus a 3-deep coverage. When on back side, run the crease and block in the deep middle (block the near safety).

TE/FLEXED END- Play Side: Block #3 when in Tight: Crack Block inside when Flexed. Back Side: Run the back side crease with intimidation of Crack Block into an outside linebacker.

PST- Block the #2 defender from the A-gap (lineman or linebacker).

PSG- Block the #1 defender (lineman or linebacker; A-gap, over, or outside).

C- Play Side Track: Cut off gap/linebacker (LB). If a nose guard/defensive lineman (NG/DL) is not present, or if the NG slides toward the BSG when Combo Blocking, release to 2nd level and block middle linebacker (MLB) or back side linebacker (BSLB).

BSG- Down Lineman Zone (DLZ): Block defensive lineman (DL) in the A-gap, over, or back side. Lock up, chop steps, rotate hips inside, and squeeze into inside gap. If Combo Blocking with center, engage NG/BSLB.

BST- Rake and Release (R & R): Rake near forearm under the adjacent shoulder pad of opponent in the B-gap, over, or back side, and then release into 2nd level to block the outside linebacker (OLB).

PERSONNEL CONSIDERATIONS- The fullback should be a quick, rugged runner with strong legs and with the capability to "break" off his up front blocking.

STRATEGY- Use when the linebackers begin to become "tailback conscious" in their defensive commitment to take-away the I-back plays, especially the **Sweep**. It is very useful as a change-up play—and it attacks the heart of the defense.

(6) The **Spike Option** is the simplest option play to execute in football. The play's initial fake to the fullback, just inside the guard, helps to "freeze" and momentarily pull the defense inward. When the fullback's thrust begins to restrain defensive pursuit, a quarterback/tailback two-way "keep-or-pitch" option "read" can be made without great difficulty against the on side defensive end. Mechanically, the quarterback uses his reverse-pivot footwork to execute both the **Spike** and the **Spike Option** plays. The purpose of the reverse-spin is to gain the depth needed to (A) Delay the defensive response to the fullback's plunge by creating doubt as to whether he is the designated ball carrier, (B) Hide the football partially from the linebackers and, perhaps, slow the process of their play recognition, (C) Attack the inside shoulder of the defensive end on the option phase so that he can be literally forced into making an immediate commitment either to engage the quarterback or to cross the scrimmage line and cover the tailback as a possible option-pitch runner, and (D) Establish the effective, though generally safe, **Quick Pass** to any loosely-covered receiver (refer to pass diagram section).

To insure consistency and simplicity-of-execution in option-play application and philosophy, the quarterback should think in terms of pitching the football, first, and turning up the field as a runner, second.

Play Name: SPIKE OPTION

ASSIGNMENTS & TECHNIQUES + PERSONNEL REQUIREMENTS & STRATEGY

QB- Pivot-step from center and execute a jab fake to the fullback directly behind the center, at an approximate depth of one yard. At the completion of the pivot, freeze momentarily with shoulders held perpendicular to the scrimmage line. The feet should be near parallel and about twelve inches apart as the fullback makes his approach behind the play side guard for his play fake. The hand-off fake should be executed with a quick jab motion toward the fullback's stomach, using both hands for ball security. As the fullback clears, run a straight track for tile inside shoulder of the on side defensive end and prepare to pitch the football to the tailback at any moment (be alert for a crash charge from the defensive end). Since the **Spike Option** is a double option play in reality, it is suggested that the quarterback think in terms of pitching the football to the tailback, first, and "turning up" into the C-gap on his keeper, second. Sizeable gains will come when the defense gets "caught up" in a chase to the pitch man, and inadvertently leaves the inside vulnerable to the quarterback's cut-back run.

TB- Counter-step, then run an option-pitch course to maintain a pitch-relationship distance of four yards in depth from the quarterback and four yards to his outside. Be alert for a pitched ball from the quarterback at the first moment the play begins. If the quarterback progresses along the line and turns up in the C-gap area, turn up the field with him to maintain a pitch relationship. If the quarterback separates from you by cutting across-the-grain, seek the most realistic defensive threat to the runner and then function as an interference blocker!

FB- Explode from stance, taking the first step with the on side foot. Keep the shoulders low, drive forward with a low center of gravity, and accept the ball fake with inside elbow up. "Sink" your inside shoulder during the fake hand off from the quarterback, and enter the B-gap with helmet and shoulder pads leaning forward during the plunge into the line. If not tackled, become a blocker—a block upon a linebacker is invaluable.

SB- Block the Pitch Support, which is the Outside Linebacker or Strong Safety (covering defensive back). Back Side: Secure the C-gap and block in deep middle. Gap Call: Block the end man on the line (EMOL).

SE- Force Block the corner back—run him up the field as deep as he will go, then "break down" into a semi crouch. Block him nose-to-nose with an uplifting whip of the hands under his shoulder pads, and sustain contact by keeping the feet churning feet. When on back side, run the crease and block in deep middle area.

TE/FLEXED END- Play side: Block either the outside linebacker or corner back. Back side: Run the back side crease with the intimidation of a Crack Block.

PST- Block the #2 defender from the center (lineman or linebacker).

PSG- Block the #1 defender from the center (lineman or linebacker).

C- Play Side Track: Cut off gap/linebacker (LB). If a nose guard/defensive lineman (NG/DL) is not present, or if the NG slides toward the BSG when Combo Blocking, release into 2nd level and block middle linebacker (MLB) or back side linebacker (BSLB).

BSG- Down Lineman Zone (DLZ): Block defensive lineman (DL) in the A-gap, over, or back side. Lock up, chop steps, rotate hips inside, and squeeze into inside gap. If Combo Blocking with center, engage NG/BSLB.

BST- Rake and Release (R & R): Rake near forearm under the adjacent shoulder pad of opponent in the B-gap, over, or back side, and then release into 2nd level to block the outside linebacker (OLB).

PERSONNEL CONSIDERATIONS- The quarterback is not required to execute triple-option manipulations, but must be capable of pitching the football accurately to the tailback, who, in turn, must be an adequate sideline runner.

STRATEGY- Use to keep defense honest, and at any time a wide play is needed.

If an offensive coordinator wishes to run a triple (veer) option rather than a double (dive) option, the following guidelines are offered ...

(A)   As a prerequisite, make certain that (1) a "reflex athlete" is available on the squad that can manipulate a three-way option, usually under immense defensive pressure, and that (2) the offensive staff is prepared to put in a tremendous amount of time for the development of this sophisticated play.

(B)   The quarterback must use a Direct (Open) Step to the play side and "reach back" with his arms and play side foot while placing the football on the belt buckle of the approaching fullback. The fullback's running "landmark" is the buttocks of the play side guard, but should make an outside "veer" cut behind his guard when he receives the football (first option).

(C)   With the football held firmly with both hands, the quarterback "rides" with the fullback's forward momentum as he embraces the ball with a soft "arm fold" (inside elbow upward). The quarterback keeps "split vision" with both his fullback and "read key" (the first down-lineman over or outside the play side tackle). At the instant the quarterback's arms are parallel to the line, he makes an instinctive "read" either to leave the football in the fullback's arm-and-stomach pouch, or to keep the football, or pitch it to the tailback (apply the same fullback and tailback techniques that relate to the Spike and Spike Option).

(D)   Whereas the play side tackle is instructed to release *either* inside or outside a covering down-lineman in order to block the inside linebacker, two down-linemen usually will be left unblocked on the line-of-scrimmage. The inside lineman that is left unblocked is designated as the "read key" and the unblocked outside lineman (defensive end or outside linebacker) is designated as the "pitch (option) key." With this having been stated, it is the quarterback's assigned duty to "GIVE" the football to the fullback on the inside (dive) read if the "read key" does ANYTHING other than attack the fullback! For example, if the "read key" waits, comes straight across the line, or charges at an angle toward the quarterback, the football is given IMMEDIATELY to the fullback on his plunge through the line. Some coaches go so far as to include a hand-off read in accordance to the pre-snap position of the shoulder pads of the "read key" (if the shoulder pads are squared to the line, the ball is left in the fullback's stomach on the "give" read; if the "read key's" pads are turned inward, the quarterback should anticipate a "keep" during his pre-snap read).

(E)   Whenever the football is "pulled back" from the fullback's stomach, the quarterback then must be prepared to contend with some sort of outside maneuver from the defense. If the pitch key takes a "box" maneuver to contain the tailback (option-pitch runner), the quarterback then must respond by "keeping" the football (his second option) and make a turn up the field, usually inside the pitch key in the C-gap area. If the pitch key should crash toward the quarterback, the football must be pitched to the trailing tailback (third option), who must maintain a depth and width of four-yards.

INSIDE-VEER BLOCKING APPLIED + RUNNING SITUATIONS

Play side Tackle's Release Angles to Block Inside Linebacker.

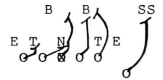 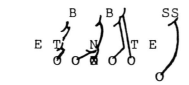 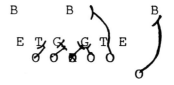

| PST must take outside release to block the ILB when read-key is aligned head-up. | PST can take an inside release to block the ILB when read-key is aligned outside. | PST can take an inside release to block the ILB when read-key is aligned to inside (can also block down on read-key, if instructed). |

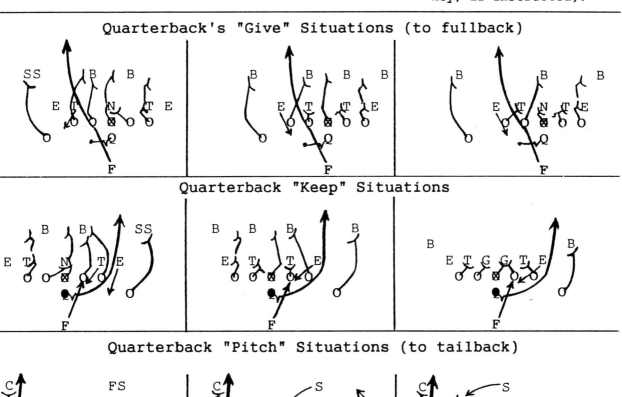

Quarterback's "Give" Situations (to fullback)

Quarterback "Keep" Situations

Quarterback "Pitch" Situations (to tailback)

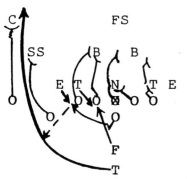 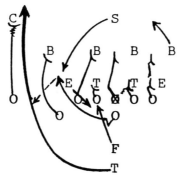 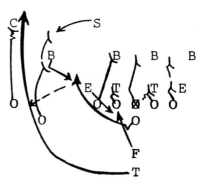

(7) The tailback **SLANT** is a contributive play that helps to blend the run/pass structure of the Flex-I/Offset offense. The blocking scheme of the **SLANT** is designed to open up a running lane just outside the play side tackle in a similar way to the traditional off-tackle Power play, which features a double-team block at the point-of-attack, and, also, to a Sprint-Draw play, which oftentimes uses special blocking schemes. The backfield timing of the latter usually is the most beneficial to a running back who is scanning for a defensive soft spot whenever the off-tackle running lane does not appear to open up. The **SLANT** play, in parallel to a Sprint-Draw, usually will confront loose-playing linebackers because of their pass coverage responsibility. The defensive ends may sometimes sacrifice an off-tackle play in their effort to contain wide runs, and the perimeter may soften their corner support in their commitment to cover all levels of pass defense. For the reasons just stated, physically-light athletes are usually better suited for a Sprint-Draw scheme rather than a Power off-tackle scheme whereas blocking force is more important. The down (angle) blocking scheme of the **SLANT** off tackle, however, can help lightweight athletes to make use of a different version of the power-blocking principle to open-up the off-tackle running lane.

An additional blocking scheme also can be applied easily and with simplicity by utilizing area or numerical-count blocking at the play side and then make use of the fullback as a lead blocker through the off-tackle hole for a tailback lead play. The tailback Lead play has characteristics that are similar to a Sprint Draw scheme, but the play side tight end/slot back will usually turn-out his usually-troublesome defensive end. This turn-out blocking effort is aided, somewhat, by the quarterback's footwork when he simulates a roll-out passing technique.

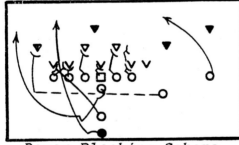

Power Blocking Scheme.

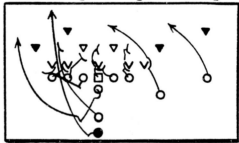

Sprint-Draw Scheme
with down-blocking.

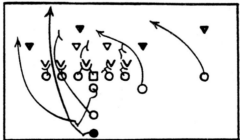

Lead Blocking Scheme with
area-rule blocking.

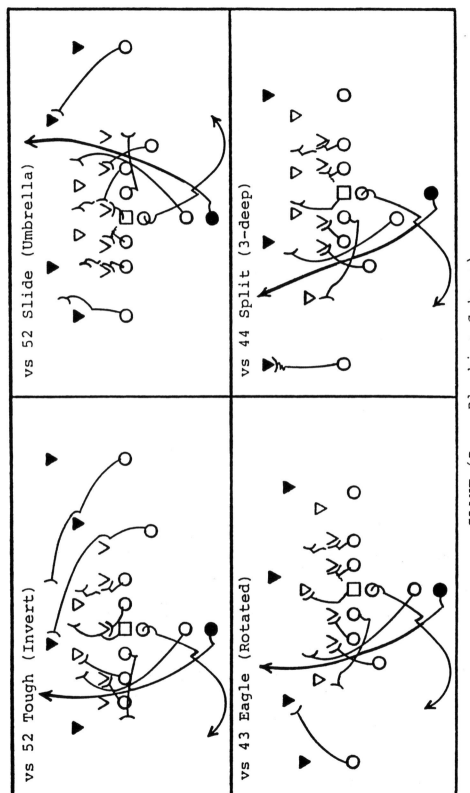

vs 52 Tough (Invert)

vs 52 Slide (Umbrella)

vs 43 Eagle (Rotated)

vs 44 Split (3-deep)

SLANT (Down-Blocking Scheme)

Play Name: SLANT

ASSIGNMENTS & TECHNIQUES + PERSONNEL REQUIREMENTS & STRATEGY

QB- Execute a Pivot Step exit from the center and run directly for the roll-out arc-pocket, whose "fish hook curve" is designed for a depth of six yards behind the on side guard. While en route to this area, make a crisp, deep hand-off to the tailback, striving for four yards in depth. The tailback's footwork prior to the hand off, incidentally, is very similar to his blitz-blocking approach that he takes toward the play side B-gap on a designated roll-out pass. After completing the hand-off, and subsequently clearing behind the tailback, continue to complete the six-yard arc and run the track of a roll-out ritual. Success with the **Slant** will enhance the effectiveness of the passing attack.

TB- Take a lateral step to the play side with the on side foot, and follow alongside with an inside-and-up step with the back side foot. Next, take a direct step with the on side foot directly ahead and receive the football from the quarterback about four yards deep in the backfield. While on-the-run toward the B-gap, prepare to "slant" into the C-gap running lane. As the play side guard opens up the off-tackle lane with his trap block, sway outward just outside the lead-blocking fullback, turn up the field inside the trap block, and then sprint through the hole.

FB- Lead Block into the inside linebacker through the play side C-gap, just outside the inside Down Block of the slot back or tight end.

SB- Down Block the first opponent aligned to the inside.   Back Side: Secure the C-gap and block in the deep middle.

SE- Play side: Sprint toward and block the near safety versus a 4-deep, and use Force Blocking tactics against a corner back versus a 3-deep coverage. When on back side, run through the coverage crease and block in deep middle.

TE- Play side: Down Block the first opponent aligned to inside.   If flexed, Crack Block into outside linebacker.
    Back side: Run the crease (if flexed, intimidate outside linebacker).

PST- Down Block the first opponent aligned to the inside.

PSG- Pull from the line to the play side and Trap Block the first defender aligned outside the slot back or tight end, from the inside-out. If trapping to flexed end side, a "short trap" will occur in the B-gap area.

C- Play Side Track: Cut off gap/linebacker (LB). If a nose guard/defensive lineman (NG/DL) is not present, or if the NG slides toward the BSG when Combo Blocking, release into 2nd level and block middle linebacker (MLB) or back side linebacker (BSLB).

BSG- Down Lineman Zone (DLZ): Block defensive lineman (DL) in the A-gap, over, or back side. Lock up, chop steps, rotate hips inside, and squeeze into inside gap. If Combo Blocking with center, engage NG/BSLB.

BST- Rake and Release (R & R): Rake near forearm under the adjacent shoulder pad of opponent in the B-gap, over, or back side, and then release into 2nd level to block the outside linebacker (OLB).

PERSONNEL CONSIDERATIONS- The tailback should be a clever, durable, and hard-nosed runner who can effectively slip into the running lane created by the linemen's trap-blocking scheme.

STRATEGY- Use as "reality check" when the defense becomes preoccupied with the passing attack. It is a good pass-situation play and deserves consideration in 3rd down and medium-yardage situations.

A POWER-DRAW VARIATION OF THE SLANT PLAY
(Enhances Turnback Pass Protection)

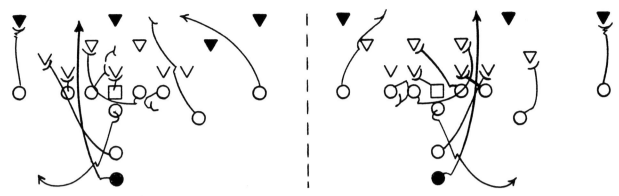

Blocking Scheme: FB--Kick-Out Block the on side end; SE- Play Side: Force Block the corner support; Back Side: run the crease and block the near safety; SB- Play Side: arc release to block the pitch support; Back Side: run the back side crease (intimidate a down block); TE/Flexed End- Play Side: block the corner support; Back Side: run the back side crease (intimidate a Crack Block); PST--identify, then block the defensive tackle with Hit technique; PSG--block the A-gap to the 2nd level; Center--block lineman aligned "over," or fill the back side A-gap; BSG--pull from line and Lead Block the linebacker aligned play side; BST--protect the inside, pivot, then shield the back side.

- -

(8) The **COUNTER** (Cross Buck) **REVERSE** is both efficient and safe as a wide play. Unlike most reverse plays, however, the development of the **Counter Reverse** unfolds with maximum quickness, thus decreasing its vulnerability to disruptive line penetrations, or to a devastating fast recovery from the opponent's secondary. Two outstanding advantages of the **Counter Reverse** are (A) The play holds the interior defense in a lull during the quarterback's manipulation of his cross-buck faking with the fullback and tailback, and (B) The play usually will turn its corner of destination with greater speed than typical wide-reverse plays. As a misdirection play, the **Counter Reverse** seems to have the same deceptive effect that the pioneer double-reverse plays had on the defenses in their era, but, in comparison, the **Counter Reverse** is neither slow in its development, nor is the timing factor as critical. The faking sequence for the quarterback, in general terms, is to (A) <u>Spin</u> <u>deep</u> from center toward the slot side, (B) <u>Jab</u> <u>fake</u> to the fullback and again to the tailback, and then (C) Follow-up with an extension of the football to the slot back for the ball exchange. In capsule, *"spin deep, double jab fake, and then extend the ball."*

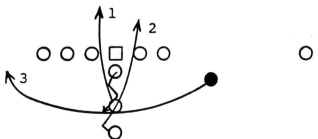

Backfield Sequence

vs 52 Slide (Umbrella)

vs 44 Split (3-deep)

vs 52 Tough (Invert)

vs 43 Eagle (Rotated)

COUNTER REVERSE

-42-

Play Name: COUNTER REVERSE

ASSIGNMENTS & TECHNIQUES + PERSONNEL REQUIREMENTS & STRATEGY

QB- Execute a deep spin from center--similar to the Pivot Step—toward the slot side of the formation. During the spin-around, make a jab fake to the fullback with the least-possible hesitation while his plunge is made into the play side A-gap. A second jab fake from quarterback to tailback then transpires after the tailback completes his counter step and starts to drive toward the back side guard-tackle B-gap to seal the hole from imminent defensive penetration. The quarterback, in a cursive flow, now proceeds with his ball exchange to the slot back while he treks through the seam of the fullback/tailback's pre-play alignment.

TB- Take a lateral step to the back side with the on side foot, and follow-up with a slide step while maintaining a slight bend in the knees. Then drive directly for the back side A-gap, opposite the fullback. Drop the inside shoulder as the quarterback indicates his jab fake, and then seal the hole.

FB- Step with on side foot, drive toward the play side A-gap, drop the inside shoulder to simulate a hand-off reception, and then seal (plug) the hole.

SB- Take a drop-step with on side foot, and run for the pre-snap seam between the fullback and tailback. Receive the handoff behind center, sprint outside the Crack Block of the flexed end and then accelerate up the sideline.

SE- Run through coverage crease and block in deep middle.

TE/FLEXED END- Tight End: Down Block the first opponent aligned to the inside. If flexed, Crack Block into the outside linebacker (OLB).

PST- Down Block the first opponent aligned to the inside.

PSG- Pull from the line, get depth, and Log Block the on side defensive end. If the tight end is flexed, the defensive end may "slide down" just outside the offensive tackle, which makes the Log Block attempt occur much closer to the inside (the joint blocking scheme of the guard and tackle now will have a similar appearance to a cross-block, except for the angle of the Log Block).

C- Block the Covering Down-Lineman: if not applicable (N/A), Fill Block into the back side A-gap.

BSG- Pull behind the center and Lead Block into the corner back on the flexed end side.

BST- Down Lineman Zone (DLZ): Block the down lineman in the B-gap, over, or back side. Lock-up, chop steps, rotate hips inside, and squeeze into inside gap. Do not allow inside penetration!

PERSONNEL CONSIDERATIONS- Both guards are required to pull from the line as escort blockers. The play side guard, therefore, must possess the agility to "pull out" and Log Block the on side defensive end. The back side guard must possess the quickness to pull from the scrimmage line, sprint on a parallel course to the flexed end side and then Lead Block into the defending corner back. The slot back should possess the necessary speed to turn the corner effectively and, thereby, become a productive sideline runner.

STRATEGY- Use when the defense shows a tendency either to pinch their line or collapse their linebackers inward when an inside play is run into the line.

PLAY	CENTER	PSG	PST	PSSB/PSTE	PSSE	BSG	BST	FB
WHAM (Lead Draw w/ILB Isolate)	Block Play Side Track: Cut off gap/LB. If no NG/DL, or if NG slides to play side, go to 2nd level.	Block the #1 defender on line-of-scrimmage (disregard linebacker).	Block the #2 defender on line-of-scrimmage (disregard linebacker).	SB: Block the Covering OLB or SS: The TE blocks the CB or OLB. Gap calls: SB & TE block DE.	Block CB vs 3-deep; NS vs 4-deep.	Block Down Lineman Zone: A-gap, Over, Back Side	Rake and Release: Rake B-gap to 2nd level	Lead Block play side ILB.
COUNTER WHAM (Counter Draw w/ ILB Isolate)	(guidelines above)	(guidelines above)	(guidelines above)	(guidelines above)	(guidelines above)	(guidelines above)	Pull play side and Lead Block on side ILB.	Fill the back side B-gap.
SWEEP + BOOTLEG (G-pull Scheme)	(guidelines above).	<G-Pull> Pull to on side corner, turn upfield and Kick-Out Block the OLB/SS.	<G-Pull> Block the DT aggressively.	Block the DE aggressively.	(guidelines above)	(guidelines above)	Rake & Release guidelines.	Fill Block play side B-gap
TACKLE TRAP (Middle Trap)	(guidelines above).	Block #1 defender; if trap target, Exit Block to outside.	Block the inside/middle linebacker. If LB is #1, Exit Block to outside.	TE: Block the DE. If flexed, Crack Block to inside.	(guidelines above)	(guidelines above)	Pull and Trap Block past center.	Fill Block back side B-gap.
SPIKE/ ROLL + SPIKE OPTION	(guidelines above)	Block #1 defender.	Block #2 defender.	SB: Block OLB/SS. TE: Block OLB or CB.	Force Block the CB	(guidelines above)	Rake & Release guidelines.	Runner/play fake
SLANT (Down-Block)	(guidelines above)	Pull and Trap Block the on side DE.	"Down Block" inside opponent.	"Down Block" inside opponent.	Block CB vs. 3-deep; NS vs 4-deep.	(guidelines above)	(guidelines above)	Lead Block ILB thru C-gap
COUNTER REVERSE	Block the covering Down Lineman; if N/A, fill back side A-gap.	Pull, get depth, and Log Block the DE.	(guideline above)	TE will "Down Block" inside opponent.	(guidelines above)	Pull & Lead Block the CB at TE side.	Block Down-Lineman Zone.	Fake and fill play side A-gap
Turnback Protection...	Hinge Block back side (BS) A-gap.	Hinge Block back side (BS) A-gap.	Block DT w/ aggressive 'Hit' tech.	Assigned pass route.	Assigned route.	Hinge BS A-gap.	Hinge BS C-gap.	Climb Block DE.

STRATEGY

PLAYS   FAVORED SITUATIONS

WHAM + KEEP: Use on any play down, and apply to any running
                 or passing situation. The Wham may be the most
                 versatile play in football! A **WHAM OPTION** also
                 may be included to broaden its threat to the
                 opposing defense.

COUNTER WHAM: Use in passing situations, since the play is
                 similar to a counter draw. If the linebackers
                 can be influenced to "pass drop" into their
                 coverage zone, the Counter Wham play will reap
                 big-play benefits.

SWEEP + Bootleg: Use when a big gain in yardage is needed. Use
                 the quarterback Bootleg when the back side de-
                 fensive end and supporting cast begin to show
                 an inward collapse.

TACKLE TRAP: Use when opponent's defensive pursuit of the
                 Sweep play becomes overly intense.

SPIKE: Use as a change-of-pace and short-yardage play.

SPIKE OPTION: Use as a long-gainer and third-and-long-yardage
                 play (adds pressure to coverage of perimeter).

SLANT: Use as a short-yardage play and, also, when a
                 pass play may be anticipated by the defense.

COUNTER REVERSE: Use when the defense tends to collapse inward
                 against inside running plays.

ROLL: Use as a change-of-pace and short-yardage play,
                 and, also, whenever the linebackers tend to
                 show a fast "read" pursuit against the Sweep.

General Observations

     The strategy involved in making play-call selections MUST vary from game
to game, and should be altered from situation to situation. Every offensive
coordinator/field general should have a basic set of reference guidelines to
consider in every game plan, and care should be taken to prevent a predict-
ability in making play selections, since this will give a well-prepared opponent a decisive advantage. In the strategy of football, as in warfare
combat, contests are sometimes won by an opponent with the least man power,
but has the best entrapment schemes and an availability of the best arsenal of
"weaponry." When a football team is well-drilled and mentally prepared, close
games can be won by cleverness and good tactical judgement. While it would be
foolish to rely solely on tricks and gimmicks, a coach must be prepared to "do
the unexpected" to defeat the better opponents on the game schedule.

II

PASSING ATTACK

The prescribed passing attack for the Flexing Offense is designed to be applied as an integral part of the overall attack. Since these patterns are tailored for this style of offensive attack, a chapter division at this point is not meant to infer that two separate attack mentalities exist. The Flexing Offense is devised specifically as a functional run/pass attack that will make the most of available personnel!

PASS PATTERNS

(1) The **QUICK PASS** may be the easiest pass in football to manipulate, and can be targeted effectively to any receiver. It serves as a great complement to the **Spike and Spike Option** plays, due to their look-alike appearance. It also places an irrefutable, three-dimensional stress upon the defensive perimeter by pressuring the defensive backs to honor the threat of a middle (tight) dive, a dive-option, and a dive-action "pop" pass. The quarterback's choice of receivers include the slot back, the split end, and the tight end when each of them run their passage through the man-to-man or zone-coverage creases of the defensive backs. The tailback's Swing route also is included in the form of an "outlet receiver." The **Quick Pass** is probably the most basic, reliable, and secure pass in modern football.

The split end, slot back, and the tight/flexed end have individual route options whenever the play fake is made to their aligned side. Each receiver(s) aligned on the side of the play-fake will signal first a Quick-In or a Quick-Up pass route to the quarterback (refer to Play Assignments). The receiver(s) that are aligned on the back side of the play-fake will automatically run a Crease route. As a guideline for the receivers, the route breaks are generally assigned on the military time-beat of "two," but the timing is flexible.

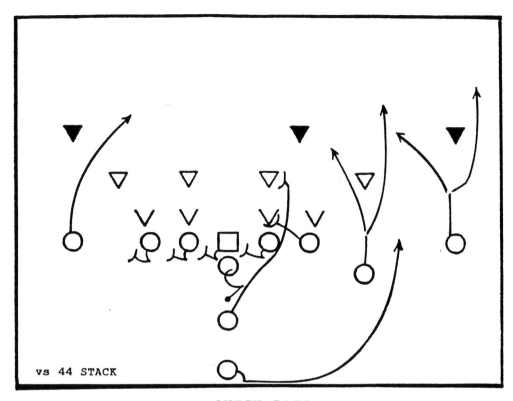

vs 44 STACK

QUICK PASS

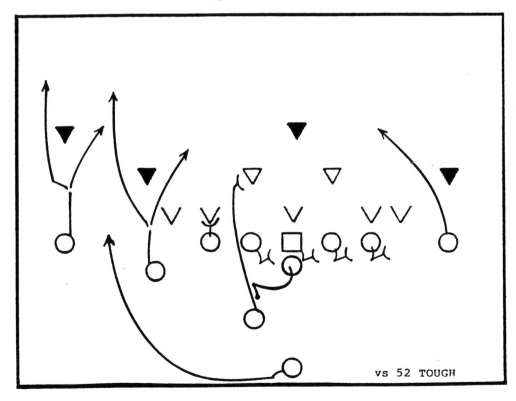

vs 52 TOUGH

Pattern Name: QUICK PASS

ASSIGNMENTS & TECHNIQUES + PERSONNEL REQUIREMENTS & STRATEGY

QB- Simulate a **Spike** play hand-off. Begin with a pivot-step to a depth of one to two yards behind the center and freeze momentarily while holding shoulders perpendicular to the scrimmage line. The feet should remain near parallel and about a foot apart while the fullback makes his approach behind the play side guard to receive the ball-exchange fake. Execute the fake with a quick jab motion toward the fullback's stomach, using both hands for ball security. As the fullback clears, take an elongated step <u>backward</u> behind the center, take a quick visual read, and then fire the ball quickly to the best choice of open-receivers.

If the **Quick Pass** is thrown off the fake of the fullback **Roll** play, use the identical footwork that is used for the running play; pivot step from center, and fake a two-handed pitch-back to the tailback at the 5 o'clock position to simulate a downhill toss sweep. Then make a jab fake to the fullback at the 3 o'clock position, take an elongated step backward behind the center, and pass the football to the best selection of open-receivers.

Since the Quick Pass is thrown about as quickly as a two-step drop "pop pass," the military time-beat of <u>two</u> is generally used for the receivers, but the timing can be modified to adjust to the depth of the covering linebackers and defensive backs. Make every attempt to release the pass just as the receivers make their timed break. The first option will consist of the receiver or receivers located on the side of the play fake (slot side or flexed/tight side), with the tailback running a Swing route.. The second option is the receiver or receivers located on the back side of the play fake, who will automatically run through the imaginary crease(s) that separate the defensive back's zone coverage(s).

TB- Run an option-pitch course, swing upward and outside the end. Be alert for a quickly-thrown "outlet" pass; may also be pre-designated as a special receiver. If a Roll play fake is specified, fake a two-handed catch as if running a sweep.

FB- Explode from stance, taking first step with on side foot. Keep shoulders low, "sink" inside shoulder during the hand-off fake, and slide outside the hip of the play side guard to occupy and blockade the inside linebacker. If a **Roll** fake is designated, carry out the footwork and arm mechanics of the play.

SB, SE, & TE/FLEXED END- Play side: Read the coverage depth, hand signal to quarterback, and run either a Quick In (slant) or Quick up (out & up) route on 2nd time-beat. Back side: Run the Crease between the corner back and outside linebacker or safety.

PST- Identify, then block defensive tackle with an aggressive Hit technique.

PSG- Hinge Block the back side A-gap (Turnback Protection).

C- Hinge Block the back side A-gap (Turnback Protection).

BSG- Hinge Block the back side B-gap (Turnback Protection).

BST- Hinge Block the back side C-gap (Turnback Protection).

PERSONNEL CONSIDERATIONS- A tall, sure-handed split end definetly is an asset. The slot back and flexed/tight also must demonstrate good receiving skills.

STRATEGY- Use whenever the **Spike Option, Roll,** or **Sweep** plays are contained, or when the defense becomes careless with its pass-coverage responsibilities.

(2) The **MISDIRECTION** pattern is a natural complement to the **Tackle Trap** play. When the outside segment of a defensive perimeter begins to reveal a preoccupation with the counter-action flow of the slot back's run through the middle, the **Misdirection** pattern is at its best advantage.

The fullback should be considered the primary receiver after he makes his slice through the guard-tackle gap and begins to run his Fan route. At this time, both the tight/flexed end and split end will begin running their In-and-Out (post-corner) routes, which first should appear as a mere cruise through their back side zone-creases before the receivers make their final cut toward their on side goal line flag. The depth of the receivers' outside breaks, before making their decisive cut toward the corner flag, is determined by the military time-beat of the pass, which normally should be designated on the count of four. The timing of all final route breaks should coincide with the pass release of the quarterback after completing his set-up in the Pull-Up pass-release pocket (techniques described in Chapter Three, entitled 'Running and Passing Game Fundamentals').

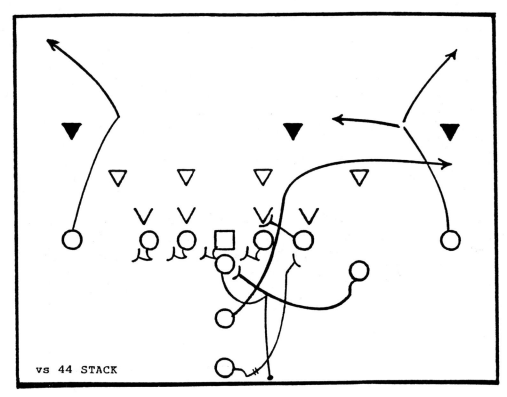

vs 44 STACK

MISDIRECTION

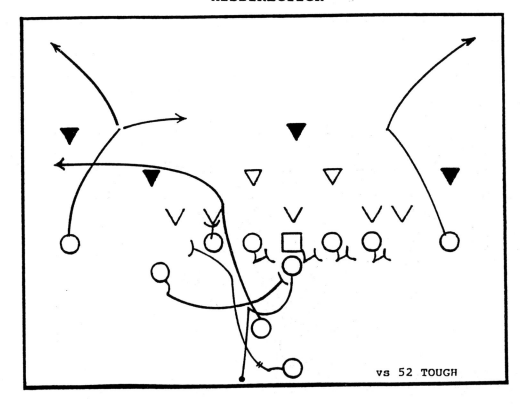

vs 52 TOUGH

Pattern Name: MISDIRECTION

ASSIGNMENTS & TECHNIQUES + PERSONNEL REQUIREMENTS & STRATEGY

QB- Take a Pivot-Step from center and fake both the tailback pitch and the "underneath" hand off to the slot back, as if running the **Tackle Trap** play. The fake ball toss to the tailback will occur at the 5 o'clock position and the follow-up fake ball exchange to the slot back will occur at the 2 o'clock position, behind the B-gap. After completing the double-fakes, retreat to the pull-up pass pocket behind the on side guard and prepare to throw to an open-receiver choice in the first option--either the fullback or the split end. If neither receiver is open, turn to the second option, the flexed/tight end, and read his availability as an open receiver. If the second-option receiver is not open, either run up the field with the football, or throw it out of bounds, or throw it into the end zone in the vicinity of an eligible receiver. Since the **Misdirection** pattern attacks horizontally in opposite directions at the on side, a military time-beat of <u>four</u> is advised for this pull-up pattern. To avoid an interception, the quarterback always should attempt to throw the football just as the receivers make their route break.

TB- Take a lateral step with slot side foot, then adjust the following steps to control-run toward the C-gap and Climb Block the defensive end from inside-to-outside, since the quarterback will set up to pass from a pull-up pocket. While en route to the C-gap area, coordinate the fake of a two-handed catch with the quarterback's ball-toss fake. A convincing ball-catching fake with the hands can help to hold the defense momentarily in a running-play mode.

FB- Lead step with on side foot, slice through the B-gap, run an arc to the outside at a depth of 6 to 7 yards on a Fan route, and then level off toward the sideline. Look immediately for the ball in flight; gather the ball with relaxed hands.

SB- Take a half-pivoting, backward step during the snap of the football to gain depth and achieve the necessary timing to mimic the Tackle Trap play. Run in front of the quarterback, accept his hand-off fake, and then seal the far side A-gap.

SE- Run a Cross route. First slant between the corner back and strong safety, then break horizontally to the inside (on the tine beat). Footwork: Widen steps before making the cut, plant outside foot, shift weight, and break inside! May also run an IN & Out (post-corner) route (described below).

TE/FLEXED END- Run an In & Out (post-corner) route. The initial slant inside should split the corner back and outside linebacker/near safety--and the break to the outside should be aimed at the corner flag. Footwork: Widen steps before cut, plant inside foot, shift weight, and break outside!

PST- Identify, then block defensive tackle with an aggressive Hit technique.

PSG- Hinge Block the back side A-gap (Turnback Protection).

C- Hinge Block the back side A-gap (Turnback Protection).

BSG-Hinge Block the back side B-gap (Turnback Protection).

BST- Hinge Block the back side C-gap (Turnback Protection).

PERSONNEL CONSIDERATIONS- A tall, sure-handed split end is an asset to this offense. The fullback should have sufficient receiver skills to catch a short pass, since he is a primary ("hot") receiver. The flexed/tight end should have average receiver skills in the least (second-option receiver).

STRATEGY- Use primarily after a succession of **Tackle Trap** plays, when the secondary is affected by the misdirection: good on 2nd down in short-yardage situations.

(3) The design of the **Waggle Pass** pattern is well suited to a quarterback bootleg with a pull-up pass pocket. To clarify the meaning of a bootleg, the quarterback will fake in one direction, and then execute his pass release in the opposite direction. This particular version of a bootleg pass, however, places the <u>back side tackle</u> in a key blocking role by pulling him from the line to the play side to contain the end man on the line (EMOL) with a Log (pin) Block if he closes inside, or with a Kick-Out (trap) Block if he steps across the line. The **Waggle Pass** employs the fullback as a *priority* receiver in its pattern by slipping him into the flat on a Fan route at the tight/flexed end side during a deceptive, counter-action play fake carried out mutually by the quarterback and tailback.

At the start of the play, the quarterback begins with a deep spin from center, nonchalantly skirts past the fullback without acknowledging his presence, and then makes a quick jab-fake motion to the tailback. This backfield action has a visual appearance, somewhat, of a traditional cross-buck play. The tailback, at the start of the play, displays an abbreviated counter step to the Tight Side, then drives for the back side guard-tackle C-gap, accepts the fake of a ball-exchange along the way, and, lastly, seals the vacated hole left by the pulling-tackle. At this time, the tight/flexed end runs a deliberate In-and-Out (post-corner) route, and the back side slot back runs a Cross route, while the split end runs a deep Mid-Line Post route.

The quarterback, meanwhile, completes his backfield ritual by pulling-up behind the Tight Side guard at a six-yard depth, views the fullback and tight/flexed end levels in his "first-option" selection, and then quickly releases his pass if the read is positive. If the first-option receivers appear covered, however, the quarterback then should turn toward the throw-back receivers in his "second option," which are the slot back and split end, and release the ball decisively to an open receiver. The military time-beat designated for the quarterback's pass release, in coordination with the route breaks of his receivers, can be set either on the count of <u>four or five</u>, depending upon the quality of the pass protection and the desired depth of the receiver routes.

The concept of the **Waggle** is to attack the opposition's perimeter coverage across its grain. This pattern can help to discourage an opponent from "loading up" its defense on the slot side of the formation with an unbalanced/overloaded coverage.

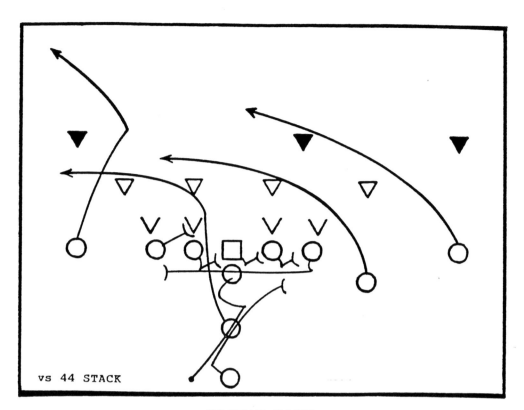

vs 44 STACK

WAGGLE PASS

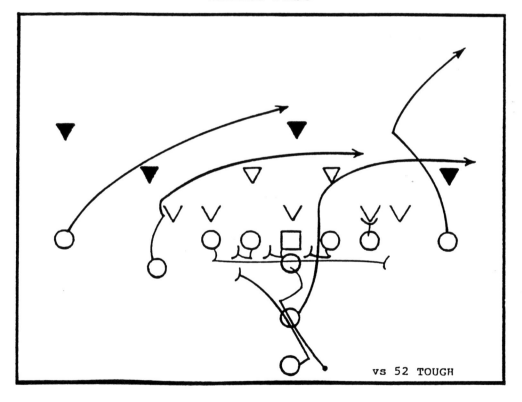

vs 52 TOUGH

Pattern: WAGGLE PASS RIGHT/LEFT

ASSIGNMENTS & TECHNIQUES + PERSONNEL REQUIREMENTS & STRATEGY

QB- Exit from center with a deep spin, similar to the technique used on the **Counter Reverse,** and jab fake to the tailback behind the Slot Side A-gap while he is going through the motions of running a counter play off tackle. After completing the jab fake, retreat to the pull-up pocket behind the Tight Side guard and prepare to throw to an open-receiver choice in the first option--either the fullback or the flexed/tight end. If neither receiver is open, turn to the second option, the slot back and the split end, and read their availability as open receiver choices (should the free safety advance up to cover the slot back, the split end will be open for a touchdown reception). If the second option receivers are not open, either run up the field with the football, or throw it out of bounds, or into the end zone in the vicinity of an eligible receiver. Since the **Waggle** attacks the "weak side" coverage with a flooding pattern, a Pull-Up Method is preferred so that a crisp, accurate pass can be thrown just as the receivers make their timed break. A military time-beat of <u>four</u> is generally recommended, but should be adjusted as needed to attack special coverages.

TB- Take a lateral step to Tight Side with the on side foot, then counter step to the Slot Side, accept the hand off fake from the quarterback, and then drive for C-gap area to seal the hole for the pulling tackle.

FB- Lead step with on side foot, slice through the A-gap, arc to the outside at a depth of 6 to 7 yards on a Fan route, and then level off toward the sideline. Look immediately for the ball in flight; gather ball with relaxed hands.

SB- Intimidate inside defender with a forearm Rake Technique, then run a Cross route at a 6-yard depth through the linebacker zone into the upper plane of the B-gap.

SE- Run a deep Mid-Line Post route; do <u>not</u> over-run the upper plane of the center.

TE/FLEXED END- Run an In & Out (post-corner) route. The initial slant to the inside should split the corner back and outside linebacker or the near safety, and the route break to the outside should be aimed at the corner flag. Footwork: Widen steps before cut, plant inside foot, shift weight, and break outside!

PST (SS)- Block the defensive tackle with an aggressive Hit technique.

PSG (SS)- Hinge Block the back side A-gap (Turnback Protection).

C- Hinge Block the back side A-gap (Turnback Protection).

BSG (TS)- Hinge Block the back side B-gap (Turnback Protection).

BST (TS)- Pull from line behind center and Log/Kick-Out Block the EMOL at play side.

PERSONNEL CONSIDERATIONS- The fullback should have short-pass receiver skills, at least, since he is a primary ("hot") receiver on this pattern. The flexed/ tight end should have adequate catching skills, as well, since he is a primary receiver. The slot back and split end must be reliable second-option receivers.

STRATEGY- Use whenever the secondary coverage is over-defending the slot side of the formation, thereby showing a disregard for the passing potential of the flexed/tight side. Recommend usage of Waggle when defensive rush from flexed/tight side is sparse.

(4) The **Wheel** pattern places tremendous vertical pressure upon all perimeter coverages. This particular version of the **Wheel** is somewhat unique because the split end has an option feature that allows him to run either a Curl or Post route, depending upon the depth of the nearest deep-playing safety. When the pattern first begins to develop, the defending corner back should sense pressure from the split end's break to the inside at the same time the slot back is slanting through his coverage zone, just prior to his quick break toward the goal line, in a full sprint.

The **Wheel** pattern is designed for a pull-up passing technique because one of the primary receivers, the split end, makes an inside route break. When the split end elects to run a Curl route, because the strong safety is playing deep and loose, the football should be thrown just as the split end makes his arc-cut into the inside zone defended by the outside linebacker or strong safety. The trajectory of the football should be brisk and direct, and thrown at the split end's face mask just as he completes his arcing turn. The catch should be made with thumbs-in, with total attention given to the airborne football.

The quarterback should avoid throwing high and over the nose bridge of curl-route receiver because of the "blind spot" between the human eyes. If and when such a pass is inadvertently thrown, however, the receiver should turn his head upward to avoid a loss of vision during the flight of the approaching ball.

When the football is thrown to a deep-route receiver, such as the split end on his Post route, and the slot back on his Rail route, the quarterback's pass should be thrown high and deep so that it can be caught while the receiver is running in a full sprint. The football should be aimed, therefore, at the inside helmet area of either deep receiver so that the ball in flight will not be difficult to catch and secure.

It is important for all receivers to learn to "look" the ball all-the-way into their hands on all receptions--and to have their fingers and hands held in a soft, relaxed cupped position (refer to Running and Passing Game Fundamentals).

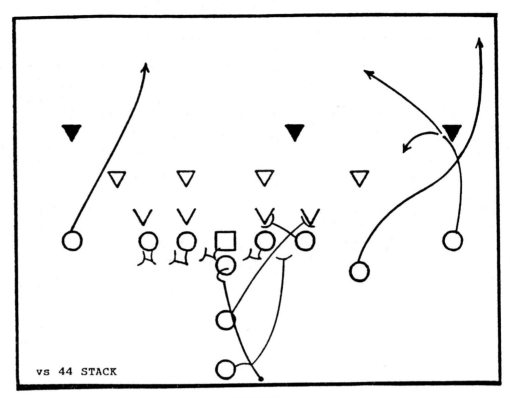

vs 44 STACK

WHEEL

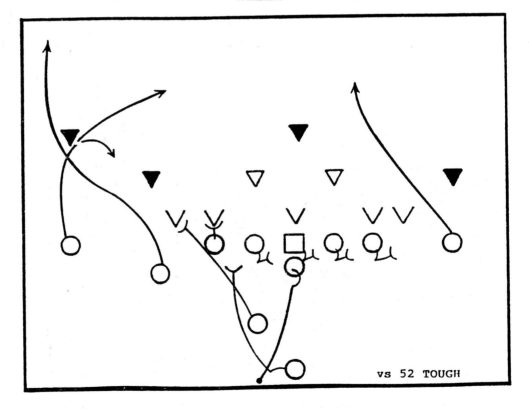

vs 52 TOUGH

Pattern Name: WHEEL

ASSIGNMENT & TECHNIQUES + PERSONNEL REQUIREMENTS & STRATEGY

QB- Exit from center with a Pivot Step. Then run to the 6-yard pull-up area behind the on side guard. The exit-retreat from center, prior to the pull-up, should first appear as the early formation of a running arc for a roll-out pass. Since the **Wheel** is a pattern that works from the outside to the inside, a Pull-Up Method is preferred so that a crisp, accurate pass can be thrown just as the receivers make their timed break. A military time-beat of <u>four</u> is recommended for this pattern, but may have to be modified at times to combat an improvised coverage devised by an opponent. When set in the pull-up pocket, read the first option, which is the split end and slot back combination, and fire the football to the best open-receiver choice of the two. If neither receiver is open, turn to the second option, the flexed/tight end, and read his availability as an open-receiver choice. If the second option receiver is not open, either run up the field with the football, or throw it out of bounds, or into the end zone in the vicinity of an eligible receiver.

TB- Take a lateral step to the play side with on side foot, follow alongside with an inside-and-up step with back side foot, and then advance forward as if a potential ball carrier. Protect the B-Gap area from leakage or a linebacker blitz.

FB- Climb Block the defensive end/end man on line (EMOL) from an inside to outside angle.

SB- Run a Rail route, which amounts to a slant-and-up combination. The "slant" phase begins with a straight-line drive for the sideline at a maximum depth of 7 yards, over the proximity of the split end's starting position. When this "proximity" is reached, break "up" the field and look for the football over the inside shoulder (timed break is on the beat of <u>four</u>). If the ball is thrown properly, it should have height and a considerable lead, so be prepared to "run for it," and to concentrate on the catching mechanics, and score!

SE- Read the depth, first, of the nearest deep safety. If he is up close, run a shallow Post route; if he is deep, run a Curl route (break on time beat of <u>four</u>). Footwork: Widen steps before cut, plant outside foot, shift weight, and break decisively!

TE/FLEXED END- Run the Crease between corner back and near safety (do not overrun).

PST- Identify, then block defensive tackle with an aggressive Hit technique.

PSG- Hinge Block the back side A-gap (Turnback Protection).

C- Hinge Block the back side A-gap (Turnback Protection).

BSG- Hinge Block the back side B-gap (Turnback Protection).

BST- Hinge Block the back side C-gap (Turnback Protection).

PERSONNEL CONSIDERATIONS- A tall, sure-handed split end is an asset to this offense. The slot back can be a shorter, craftier runner, but should also possess good pass-receiving hands. The flexed/tight end should have adequate receiver skills, at least, since he is the primary second-option receiver.

STRATEGY- Use whenever the Roll-Out patterns--whose receiver routes break outside--are challenged aggressively in the flats, which leaves the opposing secondary especially vulnereable to the **Wheel** pattern.

(5) The 'X' pattern is best used as a change-of-pace selection whenever an across-the-grain pass strike could yield either substantial yardage or a touchdown scored. The deep-crossing receivers help to explore a suspected vulnerability in the opponent's secondary coverage when the slot side of the formation is over-played. The split end's role is to run a decisive In & Out route, which will either "spring him free" behind the corner back or maneuver the corner back out of the general region that will be invaded by the crossing tight/flexed end.

Since both primary receivers are crossing in the middle, a Pull Up pass-release method is advised. The time-beat, therefore, should be on the count of <u>four</u>, but the quarterback should be permitted to have some leeway so that he can making a "timing judgement" in regard to his receiver selection and to the release of his pass. The ball should be thrown with a moderate arch and, also, should lead the receiver so that he can run to the football in it's flight.

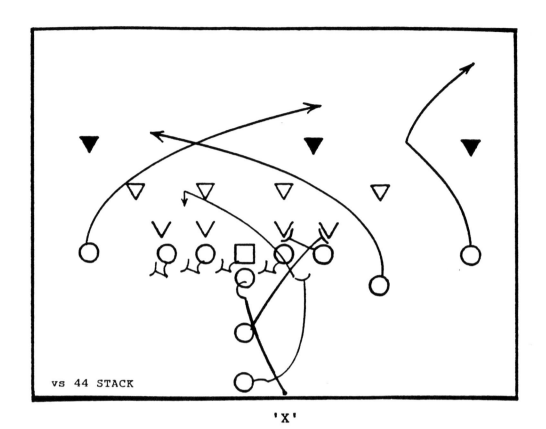

vs 44 STACK

'X'

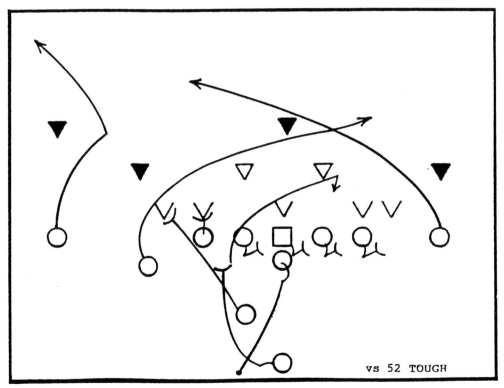

vs 52 TOUGH

Pattern Name: "X"

ASSIGNMENTS & TECHNIQUES + PERSONNEL REQUIREMENTS & STRATEGY

QB- Exit from center with a Pivot Step. Then run to the 6-yard pull-up area behind the on side guard. The exit-retreat from center, prior to the pull-up, should first appear as the early formation of a running arc for a roll-out pass. Since the "X" works as a combined inside and outside pattern, a Pull-Up Method is preferred so that a crisp, accurate pass can be thrown just while the receivers make their timed break. A military time-beat of <u>four</u> is recommended for this pattern, but may have to be modified at times to combat an improvised coverage devised by an opponent. When setting up into the pull-up pocket, read the first option, which is the flexed/tight end and split end combination, and fire the football to the best open-receiver choice of the two. If neither receiver is open, turn to the second option, the slot back and the tailback, and read their availability as open-receiver choices. If the second option receivers are not open, either run up the field with the football, or throw it out of bounds, or into the end zone in the vicinity of a receiver.

TB- Take a lateral step to the play side with on side foot, follow alongside with an inside-and-up step with back side foot, and then advance forward as a potential ball carrier. Protect the B-Gap from leakage or a linebacker blitz. If there is not any immediate pressure, slip into the linebacker zone on a Hide route, which is a "button-hook" over the back side B-Gap as a second-option receiver.

FB- Climb Block the defensive end/end man on line (EMOL) from an inside to outside angle.

SB- Run a "X" route through the inside linebacker zone, delaying slightly to allow the flexed/tight end to cross overhead, and then sprint into the target area located approximately 12 yards deep over the far side tackle.

SE- Run an In & Out (post-corner) route. The initial slant inside should be aimed to split the covering corner back and strong safety, and the outside break should be aimed at the corner flag. This course applies maximum pressure upon the covering corner back.

TE/FLEXED END- Run an "X" route, a straight course aimed at a depth of 15 yards over the slot side tackle. This course is meant to penetrate through the vulnerable far side coverage crease of the strong safety and corner back.

PST- Identify, then block defensive tackle with an aggressive Hit technique.

PSG- Hinge Block the back side A-gap (Turnback Protection).

C- Hinge Block the back side A-gap (Turnback Protection).

BSG- Hinge Block the back side B-gap (Turnback Protection).

BST- Hinge Block the back side C-gap (Turnback Protection).

PERSONNEL CONSIDERATIONS- A tall, sure-handed split end is an asset to this offense. The slot back can be a shorter, craftier runner, but should also possess good receiving hands. The flexed/tight end should have adequate receiver skills, at least, since he is a primary receiver on this pattern.

STRATEGY- Use when opponent's secondary is either over playing the slot side or using quick-response rotations to subdue the slot side patterns and flow of running plays.

(6) The **Shovel** pass is a useful "blitz breaker" against defensive units that rely heavily upon pressure tactics to disrupt their opposition's passing attack. The concept of this play lies somewhere between that of a draw play and a screen pass. Unlike a draw play, however, the **Shovel** pass is effective against a linebacker blitz, and unlike a typical middle screen, it can capitalize upon the techniques used with Turnback Blocking. Two main essentials that will determine a successful application of the **Shovel** pass are (A) The fullback's determination to carry out a forceful Kick-Out Block upon the defensive end, and (B) The tailback's disciplined usage of his footwork to display the appearance of a blitz-protecting approach to the line.

The tailback's approach angle as a would-be blocker should be altered, however, toward the inside leg of his on side tackle so that he can turn easily to his inside and face the quarterback at the crest of his pocket set up. The tailback must concentrate upon the football's brief air flight while it is flipped by the quarterback in a shoveling motion. Upon catching the football, the tailback should pivot from his posterior position, attempt to stay to the inside of his offensive tackle, face up-the-field, and size-up the situation by running through the best alleyway available between the maze of defenders.

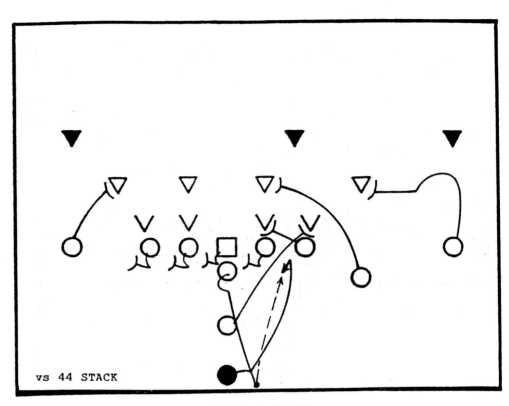

vs 44 STACK

SHOVEL PASS

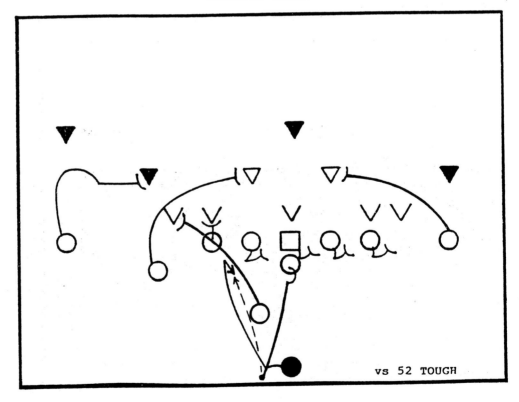

vs 52 TOUGH

Pattern Name: SHOVEL

ASSIGNMENTS & TECHNIQUES + PERSONNEL REQUIREMENTS & STRATEGY

QB- Exit from center with a Pivot Step. Then run to the 6-7 yard pull-up area behind the on side guard. When leaving the center, prior to the pull up, attempt to give the defense an impression that a Roll-Out pass attempt is in the making. Since the Shovel pass is a Draw play of sorts--with the pass-rush necessity of a Middle Screen--a pass release from the Pull-Up Method is preferred so that a soft, underhand flip of the football can be made just as the tailback makes his turnabout to catch his pass behind the B-gap. A military time-beat of four is recommended for this short, shovel-action pass. When setting up in the Pull-Up Pocket behind the on side guard, invite a pass rush and then step backward, if needed, to evade the onslaught of rushers. In a similarity to a screen pass, a strong rush will increase the play's probability of success.

TB- Take a lateral step to play side with the on side foot, follow alongside with an inside-and-up step with the back side foot, and then advance forward as if pass blocking. Upon reaching the B-gap area, pivot completely around just inside the slot side tackle and face the quarterback. Be ready for a quick underhand flip of the football from the quarterback, "look" the football into the hands during the catch, and tuck it under the inside arm. With the ball gripped securely, turn quickly to face the defense, with the ball now resting under outside arm. Size-up the situation and run through the best clearing available.

FB- Climb Block the defensive end/end man on line (EMOL) from an inside to outside angle.

SB- Shield Block the first linebacker aligned to the inside.

SE- Shield Block the most-threatening outside linebacker or strong safety.

TE/FLEXED END- Shield Block the first linebacker aligned to the inside.

PST- Identify, then block defensive tackle with an aggressive Hit technique.

PSG- Hinge Block the back side A-gap (Turnback Protection).

C- Hinge Block the back side A-gap (Turnback Protection).

BSG- Hinge Block the back side B-gap (Turnback Protection).

BST- Hinge Block the back side C-gap (Turnback Protection).

PERSONNEL CONSIDERATIONS- The tailback must be sure-handed as a short-pass receiver, have the instinct to find an opening, and then make the best of his running opportunities. The quarterback must be able to handle defensive pressure while he is preparing to flip the football to the tailback. It is essential that the fullback provide a solid block upon the defensive end, and that each receiver effectively Shield Block their innermost linebacker or safety.

STRATEGY- Apply in situations whenever a pass attempt would normally be made--which will vary with each coach and/or field general. Make an attempt, however, to use this play only when the defense is exerting pressure on the quarterback!

(7) The **Screen Pass** to the tight/flexed-end side helps to keep the pass coverage of the defense balanced and honest. This type of pass can be especially useful when counter-attacking defensive teams that show a tendency to crash their ends, slant their tackles, and/or direct various linebacker blitzes into the tight/flexed end side of the formation (where fewer potential pass receivers are present). The outside **Screen Pass** is "made-to-order" for <u>Turnback</u> <u>Pass</u> <u>Protection</u> techniques since it helps to disguise the intent of it's three key blockers--the play side tackle, guard, and the center--who block momentarily with Turnback Pass Blocking techniques before releasing into their blocking wall. Turnback Protection, thereby, does not give the defense a preliminary tip-off to the developmental process of the **Screen Pass**, which is an praiseworthy attribute in itself.

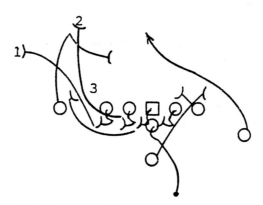

Blocking Sequence of Screen Wall (1,2,& 3)
-PST, PSG, and Center Hinge Block 3 Seconds
before releasing into the "Screen Wall"-

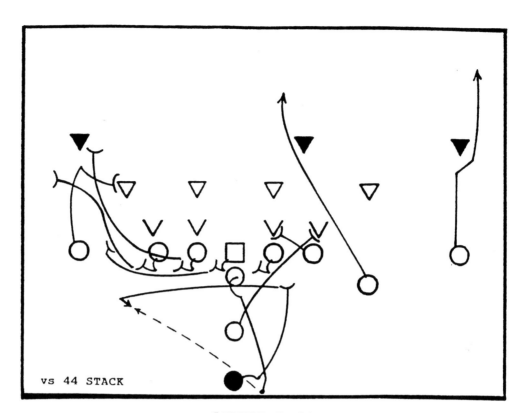

vs 44 STACK

SCREEN PASS

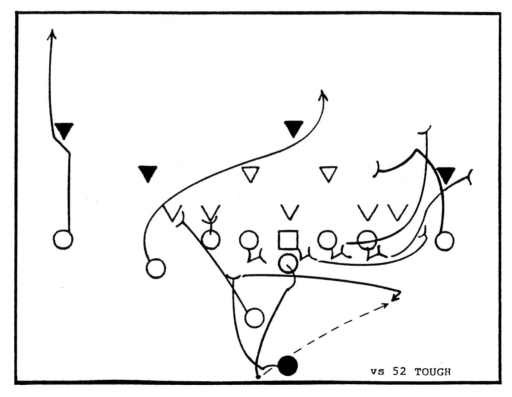

vs 52 TOUGH

Pattern Name: SCREEN PASS LEFT/RIGHT

ASSIGNMENTS & TECHNIQUES + PERSONNEL REQUIREMENTS & STRATEGY

QB- Exit from center with a Pivot Step. Then run to the 6-7 yard pull-up area behind the on side guard. When leaving the center, prior to the pull up, attempt to give the defense an impression that a Roll-Out Pass attempt is in the making. Since the **Screen** is structured as a behind-the-line pass to the tailback, who is protected by a moving wall of blockers, a Pull-Up Method is preferred so that a crisp, accurate pass can be thrown on a three-second silent count of "one thousand three." It is important to look up the field during the pocket set up and attempt to bait the defense into a hard pass rush. An intense rush would justify an additional retreat backwards for two or three steps, thus drawing the defensive charge deeper into the backfield. The defense must be sold on the deep-pass intent of the offense, otherwise the screen pass effort will fail. When the on side linemen break to their outside and begin forming their screen wall, the tailback will begin to slide into his pass-receiving position--about 4 yards outside the play side tackle's line-up position, and 2 yards behind the line. At this time, turn toward the tailback and pass the football directly to him with a "soft touch".

TB- Take a lateral step play side with the on side foot, follow alongside with an inside-and-up step with the back side foot, and then advance forward as if pass blocking. Pretend to protect the B-gap area from a blitz and/or line leakage, but "lose the block" when penetration occurs to "allow" the rushing defenders to get through the pass protection. After the 3-second count of "one thousand three," release to the opposite side behind the line--and behind the defensive penetration--to begin setting up four yards outside the play side tackle's line-up position, facing the quarterback at a depth of two yards. Give the "BALL" command when the pass is caught and <u>follow behind the blocking surge of screen-wall blockers!</u>

FB- Climb Block the defensive end/end man on line (EMOL) from an inside to outside angle.

SB- Drive for inside shoulder of the free safety and occupy him at mid field.

SE- Drive for the corner back and take him deep with an up route break.

TE/FLEXED END- Play Side: Advance toward the corner back, then Shield Block inside to block first linebacker to appear. Back Side call: Block the inside linebacker (ILB).

Tight Side Tackle- Hinge Block for 3 seconds, release outside to establish screen wall and then block corner back on "BALL" command from the tailback.

Tight Side Guard- Hinge Block for 3 seconds, release outside--keeping 4-5 feet inside the on side tackle--and then Lead Block up the field on tailback's "Ball" command.

Center- Hinge Block for 3 seconds, release outside and seal the critical area inside the on side guard, and then surge up the field on tailback's "BALL" command.

Slot Side Guard- Hinge Block inside toward the A-gap (Turnback Protection).

Slot Side Tackle- Block the defensive tackle with an aggressive Hit technique.

PERSONNEL CONSIDERATIONS- Teamwork and timing is the key--little else matters.

STRATEGY- Use on any down-and-distance situation and at any field position when an intense pass rush is anticipated. The 35 degree Turnback Protection angles are perfect for this screen pass--it is an awesome play when the <u>components</u> are well <u>coordinated</u> and the up field blocking surge is made in <u>unison</u>!

(8) The **Divide** pattern is especially suited for a roll-out passing attack, since it attacks the flats safely and reliably. It is also a great "clutch" pass that an offensive team can be depend upon in ball-control situations. It's name can be associated with the wide receiver's attempt to "divide" the coverage area of the corner back and strong safety by making a methodical, sharp cut toward his sideline on an Out route. While the split end is making his outside cut, the slot back must release from his stance in a full sprint and drive in a hard, straight line for the goal-line flag.

At the onset of the pattern, the initial attempt of the receivers is to place the corner back in a situational bind whereas he has to "take-on" two receivers at once and, therefore, be confronted with an instantaneous decision to cover one receiver and allow the other to go free. His decision choice, therefore, is whom to cover, the out-breaking split end or the approaching slot back who first should appear to be running a Slant route. If the defensive coverage is structured to protect the corner back from getting into such a "decision-making bind," the slot back may elect to run straight up-field, first, to force the deep-covering safety to retreat backward, and then make a decisive cut for the goal line flag.

The designated second-option receiver is the tight/flexed end, who is assigned to run a Cross route through the linebacker zone, which, at times, will open-up late in the pattern. Since the **Divide** pattern is designed primarily for a Roll Out passing method, the military time-beat break for the receivers should be set on the count of <u>five</u>, but the quarterback should be given some flexibility in releasing the football on his own timing, since he is applying pressure on the outside perimeter of the defense--which must also defend against a possibility of his forward advance as a potential runner.

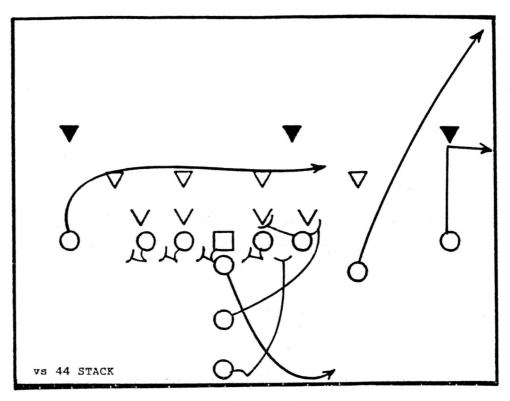

vs 44 STACK

DIVIDE

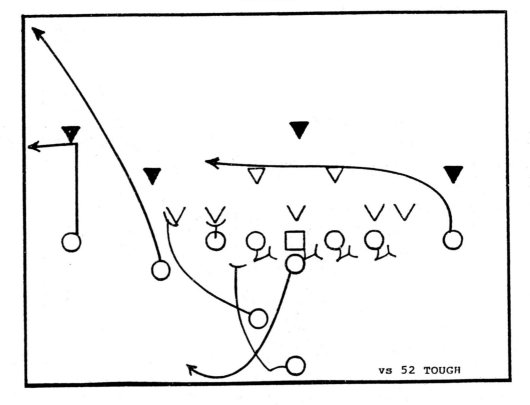

vs 52 TOUGH

Pattern Name: DIVIDE

ASSIGNMENTS & TECHNIQUES + PERSONNEL REQUIREMENTS & STRATEGY

QB- Execute a Pivot Step exit from the center and begin to run the 6-yard "fish hook" arc that is essential to a successful Roll-Out pass. Running the arc properly, which should peak behind the on side guard, will help to insure a crisp execution of a well-thrown pass, since the shoulders will be facing the receiver-group of the first option during the pass delivery. A Roll Out passing method is used with the **Divide** pattern because (1) All first-option receivers challenge their flank coverage, (2) Fewer problems arise during pass protection, and (3) Fewer pass-interception incidents occur. The standard military time-beat for the receivers on all roll-out patterns is five, but the quarterback usually has some leeway in throwing on his own timing. When running the arc, angle toward the outside, read the first option--which is the split end and slot back combination--and pass the football to the best open-receiver choice of the two. If neither receiver is open, turn to the second option--the flexed/tight end--and read his availability as an open-receiver choice. If the second option receiver is not open, either run up the field with football, or throw it out of bounds, or overthrow it into end zone.

TB- Take a lateral step to play side with the on side foot, follow alongside with an inside-and-up step with back side foot, and then advance forward as a potential ball carrier. Protect the B-gap area from leakage or linebacker blitz.

FB- Climb Block the defensive end/end man on line (EMOL) from an outside to inside angle.

SB- Run a Flag route, which consists of a hard-sprinting, straight-line drive for the goal-line flag. If the near safety is "hugging close" in man coverage, run him straight backward before driving for the goal-line flag. Look for the thrown football over the outside shoulder on the fifth time-beat.

SE- Run an Out route, which consists of a sharp 45 degree break toward the sideline on the fifth time beat. To execute the break, bring the body's weight under control prior to the outside cut, first by widening the steps and then by planting the inside foot--in conjunction with an inside head feint--before pushing-off forcefully to the outside. A snap of the elbows to the outside also helps to sharpen the shift of weight to the outside. Look for the thrown football at chest level near the outside jersey number, but adjust accordingly.

TE/FLEXED END- Run a Cross route, which is a near-horizontal trek through the linebacker zone, within the "scan" of the quarterback during his roll-out. To execute, slant through the crease of the corner back and outside linebackers, then plant and push-off on the outside foot to run the route.

PST- Identify, then block defensive tackle with an aggressive Hit technique.

PSG- Hinge Block the back side A-gap (Turnback Protection).

C- Hinge Block the back side A-gap (Turnback Protection).

BSG- Hinge Block the back side B-gap (Turnback Protection).

BST- Hinge Block the back side C-gap (Turnback Protection).

PERSONNEL CONSIDERATIONS- A tall, sure-handed split end is an asset to this offense. The slot back can be a shorter, craftier runner, but should also possess good receiving hands. The flexed/tight end should have adequate receiver skills, at least, since he is the primary second-option receiver.

STRATEGY- Use as a ball-control pass on any down-and-distance situation or at any time during the game. The **Divide** is a great pattern to use in a "two-minute offense" game plan!

(9) The **Split** pattern associates its name with the slot back's attempt to split the coverage zone of the strong safety and corner back, either with a sharp cut on an Out route, or a hard driving Slant route through the outside "underneath" zone, whose ceiling is usually 8-10 yards in depth. While this action is taking place, the split end runs an Up (fade) route that is near parallel to the sideline. This simultaneous action by the two on side receivers places the corner back, again, in a "bind" as whether to "hang close" in the underneath coverage zone or to "run" with the up-breaking wide receiver.

The tight/flexed end, again, will run a late-opening Cross route through the linebacker zone, since this is his usual assignment on Roll-Out passes. The **Split** pattern is meant to work in close coordination with both the **Divide** and the **Wheel** patterns--when one of the three is "taken away" by the opponent's pass-defense coverage, usually one or both of the remaining patterns will open-up, theoretically, when called into service. If this axiom does not hold true, the run-support of the defense may reveal a vulnerability to end runs, when probed. The three patterns mentioned above also are adaptable to a *tailback Sweep Pass*.

The quarterback's decision to pass first, and run second should remain consistent for <u>all</u> Roll-Out patterns. If the quarterback should perceive that it is unwise to release the football due to an opponent's tight secondary coverage, he should then sprint up the field for running yardage.

Since the **Split** pattern is designed for a Roll Out pass delivery, the designated military time-beat for the pass release is on the count of <u>five</u>. The quarterback should be given some flexibility in timing, however, because his forward advance applies pressure on the outer perimeter of the defense and, therefore, the judgement made in the lead-distance given to the selected out-breaking receiver can be adjusted.

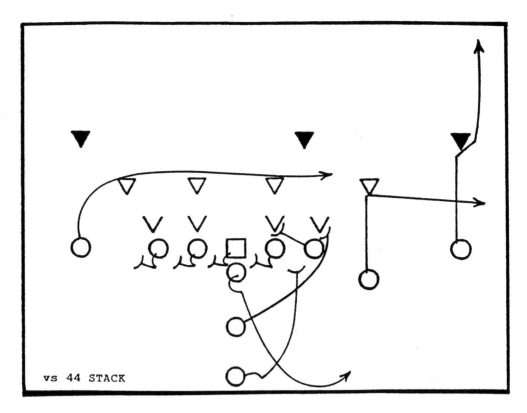

vs 44 STACK

SPLIT

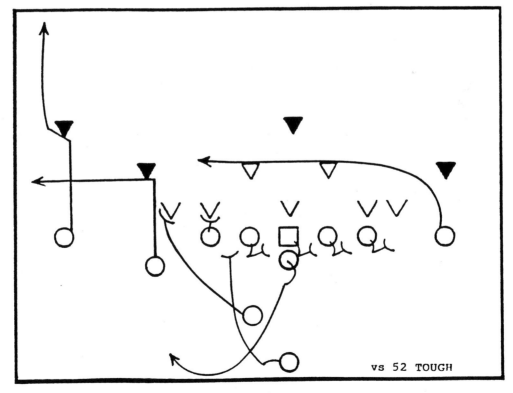

vs 52 TOUGH

Pattern Name: SPLIT

ASSIGNMENTS & TECHNIQUES + PERSONNEL REQUIREMENTS & STRATEGY

QB- Execute a Pivot Step exit from the center and begin to run the 6-7 yard "fish hook" arc that is essential to a successful Roll-Out pass. Running the arc properly, which should peak behind the on side guard, will help to insure a crisp execution of a well-thrown pass, since the shoulders will be facing the receiver-group of the first option during the pass delivery. A Roll Out passing method is used with the **Split** pattern because (1) All first-option receivers challenge their flank coverage (2) Fewer problems arise during pass protection, and (3) Fewer pass-interception incidents occur. The standard military time-beat for the receivers on all Roll-Out patterns is <u>five</u>, but the quarterback should have some leeway in throwing on his own timing. When running the arc, angle toward the outside, read the first option--which is the split end and slot back combination--and pass the football to the best open-receiver choice of the two. If neither receiver is open, turn to the second option--the flexed/ tight end--and read his availability as an open-receiver choice. If the second option receiver is not open, either run up the field with football, or throw it out of bounds, or overthrow it into end zone.

TB- Take a lateral step to play side with the on side foot, follow alongside with an inside-and-up step with back side foot, and then advance forward as a potential ball carrier. Protect the B-gap area from leakage or linebacker blitz.

FB- Climb Block the defensive end/end man on line (EMOL) from an outside to inside angle.

SB- Run an Out route, which consists of a sharp 45 degree break toward the sideline on the <u>fifth</u> time beat. To execute the break, bring the body's weight under control prior to the outside cut, first by widening the steps and then by planting the inside foot--in conjunction with an inside head feint--before pushing-off forcefully to the outside. A snap of the elbows to the outside also helps to sharpen the shift of weight to the outside. Look for the thrown football at chest level near the outside jersey number, but adjust accordingly

SE- Run an Up (fade) route. This consists of a 35 degree cut to the outside on the fourth time-beat (inside foot plant), and another cut up the sideline on the third step (outside foot plant). Look for ball from the inside, but prepare to "fade" toward the sideline for the catch if the coverage is tight.

TE/FLEXED END- Run a Cross route, which is a near-horizontal trek through the linebacker zone, within the "scan" of the quarterback during his Roll-Out. To execute, slant through the crease of the corner back and outside linebackers, then plant and push-off on the outside foot to run the route.

PST- Identify, then block defensive tackle with an aggressive Hit technique.

PSG- Hinge Block the back side A-gap (Turnback Protection).

C- Hinge Block the back side A-gap (Turnback Protection).

BSG- Hinge Block the back side B-gap (Turnback Protection).

BST- Hinge Block the back side C-gap (Turnback Protection).

PERSONNEL CONSIDERATIONS- A tall, sure-handed split end is an asset to this offense. The slot back can be a shorter, craftier runner, but should also possess good receiving hands. The flexed/tight end should have adequate receiver skills, at least, since he is the primary second-option receiver.

STRATEGY- Use as a ball-control pass on any down-and-distance situation or at any time during the game. The **Split** is a great pattern for a "two-minute offense" game plan.

III

RUNNING AND PASSING GAME FUNDAMENTALS

OBJECTIVE: The primary goal of this chapter is (1) To fortify the play assignments of the **Flexing Offense** with a modified outline of the fundamental techniques involved, and (2) To lay a foundation for the following chapters that also includes the **Multiflex** concept--which is readily adaptable to a vast variety of established offensive systems. A coverage of fundamental technique at this stage will help minimize needless redundancies and repetitions in the chapters to follow.

RUN BLOCKS

(ASSIGNMENT BLOCKING)

ORIENTATION: A development of all the fundamentals of football is crucial to winning with a consistency that will endure! Successful blocking is a critical factor in bringing reality to a team's offensive success. Achieving blocking success will ultimately narrow down to two basic essentials: (1) Explosion and (2) Sustaining Contact with Leg Drive.

PRE-SNAP:

1.   Assume a three point stance with body weight balanced. The offensive guards and tackles should align their helmets with the center's jersey numbers to give them the depth for maneuverability when attempting to cut off defensive slants, stunts, and gap stacks.

2.   Spread feet to shoulder width, pigeon-toed slightly, and taking care not to tip-off blocking assignments by looking at or leaning toward the intended target or target zone.

3.   Extend the fingers of the grounded hand to help support the applied forward pressure of the stance. The foot on the side of the grounded hand should be staggered to the rear heel of the forward foot (some coaches require their guards and tackles on both sides of center to stagger their inside foot to help expedite their steps for inside gap-control).

4.   Adjust the plane of the buttocks to a level just below the head to produce a "Power-Explosion" angle within bend of knees.

5.   Lay the free-hanging forearm over the front knee in a stabilizing position, poised to up-swing in unison with the grounded hand to make a simultaneous, double-palmed contact into the chest of the defensive opponent.

6. Focus the eyes straight ahead at a generalized area, approximately at waist level. Mentally concentrate on the attack area, since timing is essential to a blocker's control of the "penetration zone."

EXPLOSION:

1. Focus "mental weight" on the foot opposite the lead-step foot as a subconscious aid in pushing-off from the line. Swell the neck muscles for a measure of security.

2. Energize intensity and determination in preparation to explode off the line on time, at an incline angle.

3. Get "psyched up" to win the personal challenge of quickness, finesse, and cleverness over the opponent! This is essential to team victory, irrespective of one-on-one or zone blocking principles that may be applied.

4. Make a first-strike commitment on every play! Spring from a coiled stance with ultimate quickness, taking the first step with near side foot!

STRIKE and CONTINUITY:

1. Charge through the cut-off area, using the headgear as a guide post. The aim point against a head-on defender is under his chin (DRIVE BLOCK), and into his far-side jersey number when the opponent is aligned either to the inside or outside of the blocker (CUT-OFF BLOCK).

2. Strike the opponent firmly with the hands, first, then succeed with chest and shoulder contact. Be certain that a straight surge takes place from Point-A to Point-B, then square the shoulders to the scrimmage line.

3. Jolt the opponent with initial contact by exploding with an UPLIFTING WHIP OF THE ARMS, making contact with HEELS OF HANDS just under his jersey numbers.

4. Keep the hands inside and "bench press" opponent while invoking leg drive (this "total process" utilizes all skeletal muscles).

5. Execute footwork that is short, choppy and progressive! Strive for eight steps, never losing momentum by allowing a pause between follow-up steps.

6. Use piston-like steps to assure that contact with opponent is sustained. Use this technique even if a stalemate takes place, because the energy of motion will be helpful in maintaining position and control over the defender.

(ZONE BLOCKING SCHEME)

ORIENTATION: The stance, facial expression and body language of all linemen must remain the same as when they engage in one-on-one challenges. The difference in application, though, is that individual blockers are working in combinations, from inside to outside. Their intent is to cover their assigned gaps, and, also, to gain leverage when blocking their opponent within the battle zone. The first concern of all zone-blocking linemen must be to seal off the internal gaps from premature defensive penetration! *The blocker's objective is to drive through their assigned zone and attack any opponent in their pathway with a POWERING SURGE!*

Prior to the center snap of the football, zone blocking techniques are executed without taking a pre-read of any specific defenders.

PLAY SIDE ZONE BLOCKING STEPS

1.   Whenever a play side guard or tackle is "covered" by a defensive lineman, he must aim his blocking charge, initially, at the outside foot of the opponent. The blocker should first take an open step to the outside of his opponent, then take a cross-over step and attempt to "step on his opponent's outside foot" as he squares-up. He then makes an uplifting whip of the heels of his hands into the opponent's outside breast, while striving to sustain his thrust. If contact is lost because the defender slips to the inside, he must then "work upfield" to the second level and seek out a linebacker to "wall-off."

2.   The inside partner of any "blocking combo" is assigned to pick up a defensive opponent who attempts to slip between himself and his outside blocker. This process functions best if the inside blocking partner is "uncovered," which means that he is in a linebacker zone. A "scoop" blocking technique is used by the inside blocker to engage and effectively block a defender who is attempting to penetrate through the line.

3.   If a blocker's inside partner is covered, or if the defensive front is gapped, the center, and the play side guard and tackle should have a communication system to coordinate their blocking options. The choices usually are to either "reach block" their covered or gapped opponent or to apply one of their combination blocking schemes.

4.   When the play side guard is uncovered by a lineman (linebacker area), his zone block should begin with an outward depth step to achieve a somewhat stacked relationship with his tackle.

A. His second step is a short cross-over, followed by a third step that angles upfield. This third step helps the play side guard to square his shoulders to the line. Staying "squared-up" helps him to "reach" into the outside lineman without losing his opponent to the inside.

   B. At the <u>decision point</u>, the <u>guard must surge</u> his block into the linebacker if the defensive lineman slips to the outside (offensive tackle's zone). The guard can communicate with his tackle to work upfield by using a one-handed <u>shove</u> into the side of his partner.

PLAY SIDE ZONE (COMBO) BLOCKING EXAMPLES FROM BACK SET STANCES

The <u>uncovered</u> inside blocker first must step outward for depth, take a short cross-over step, and then follow-up with a squared-up surge through the blocking zone. The <u>covered</u> outside blocker first must step to the outside, take a cross-over step, and then follow-up with an attempt to "step onto the opponents outside foot," while squaring shoulders to the scrimmage line. At the moment of contact, both blockers exert an uplifting whip with the heels of their hands into their lineman's chest area. If a double team block is sustained upon the targeted defensive lineman, the opponent should be driven northward into the linebacker! If the defensive lineman should slip either to the inside or outside, the decision/reaction crossroad for the two combo blockers would then arrive, as indicated in the illustrations below.

If the defensive lineman slips outside, the inside blocker (guard) will continue to surge forward into the linebacker. The outside blocker (tackle), meanwhile, engages the opponent with a drive block.

If the defensive lineman slips inside, the inside blocker (guard) will "shove off" the outside blocker (tackle) to block the linebacker, while tying up the defensive lineman with a drive block.

BACK SIDE ZONE BLOCKING STEPS

The "universal" back side zone blocking guideline for triple-option attacks is to employ scoop blocking techniques for the center, back side guard and tackle. These linemen take an arc-step toward the on side gap as a blocking unit to occupy and seal-off the opponents who challenge the back side gaps. If and when a gap-blocker's surge clears through any of the zone gaps, the blocker should then work upward to the second level and wall-off the back side linebacker.

An altered zone blocking scheme, however, will be presented below. This altered scheme will secure the on side gaps against defensive penetration without shortening the back side C-gap area, therefore the C-gap and D-gap defenders are not sucked into a crashing charge from the outside.

1. The center blocks in the Play Side Track! He takes a tight scoop if he is covered and a wide scoop if he is uncovered. He must use his back-side forearm and shoulder to "rip" through his defender while he engages him. If his opponent slips to the inside, he then works upfield into the "second level" to wall off an unblocked, fast-flowing linebacker.

2. The back side guard blocks the Down Lineman Zone! His blocking guideline is to block the first defensive lineman to align from his inside to the back side. His technique is to lock up, chop steps, rotate hips inside, and squeeze into inside gap. If he is uncovered, he will use a scoop blocking technique that is similar to that used on the play side. His angle usually takes a flatter course, however, because he will be working in blocking combination, normally, with the center (52 defense) to seal off the nose guard, who is the "inside" down lineman in his zone.

3. The back side tackle normally will be assigned to Rake and Release! This means that he will rake (swipe) his near forearm under the adjacent shoulder pad of the first opponent to align from his inside to the back side. After the targeted defender is jolted with a forearm rake, release into the 2nd level and wall-off this area from outside pursuit.

4. In summing-up, the play side tackle and guard are generally assigned to their *nearby defensive tackle* and linebacker, the center and back side guard are responsible for the nose guard and back side linebacker, while the back side tackle is delegated to a role of scoop and cut-off from inside to the back side.

BACK SIDE ZONE BLOCKING ILLUSTRATIONS FROM BACK SET STANCES

The center is responsible for blocking through the Play Side Track. This means that he must cut off the on side gap from a penetration threat, first, then work up the field to the second level to block the middle or back side linebacker. If a nose guard or defensive lineman is not present, or if the nose guard slides toward the back side guard during their combo block, the center should then drive upward to block the linebacker.

The back side guard works in combination with the center by blocking the Down Lineman Zone. This means that he will block the A-gap first, a head-up ("over") defender second, and, lastly, the back side lineman. His scoop step, when uncovered, takes a flatter course than would the play side guard. When covered, his technique is to lock up, chop steps, rotate his hips inside, and use the buttocks to squeeze (compress) the inside gap.

The back side tackle applies the principle of Rake and Release, which means that he will "forearm rip" the adjacent shoulder pad of the defensive lineman in the B-gap first, the "over" position secondly, and the back side area lastly, before releasing to the second level to block a linebacker from his outside. *Examples are illustrated below, with an inclusion of zone blocking applications that are similar to play side inside/outside blocking combinations.*

(inside blocker scoops upward to linebacker level; outside blocker picks up outside slant)

(inside blocker picks up inside slant; outside blocker picks up linebacker flow)

Against the 4-4 and 4-3 alignments, the back side guard's "down lineman' is located either head-up or outside, which simplifies the blocking application: He locks-up with his covering opponent, chops his steps, rotates his hips in-side, and then squeezes into the inside gap. The center blocks the linebacker within the Play Side Track, while the back side tackle applies a "forearm rip" into the area opponent before releasing to second level (Rake and Release).

-
-
-
-
-
-

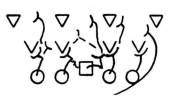

Center's Gap Control

Center can take a protective slide step into the play side A-gap when anticipating a 4-on-3 middle blitz. If gap is secure, proceed to cut-off the middle/back side linebacker. Note the important hip rotation and gap "squeeze" taken by back side guard.

PASS BLOCKING GUIDELINES

ORIENTATION: Pass Protection Blocking techniques and methods have many diverse categories. Some of the popular technique schemes include: (1) Hit (Aggressive) Protection for quick-pass action, (2) Turnback (Combination Hit & Hinge) Protection for play-action, pull-up and roll-out passes, (3) Hit and Recover (Recoil) Protection for 3-step quarterback drops, and (4) Extend and Hinge (Cup) Protection for 7-step quarterback pocket drops. Regardless of the selected pass blocking scheme, however, the fundamentals of technique must always be taken seriously, since they focus on stance, body leverage, the quick explosion of a blocker from his pre-snap stance, and the blocker's emotional and mental intensity! An abstract of pass protection guidelines and techniques for the pass blocking schemes will follow henceforth...

HIT Protection
--quick-passes--

1.   Strike quickly into the jersey numbers of the opponent covering you, with the identical techniques that would be used with an assignment block for the "run."

2.   If uncovered, lead-step into the on side gap, then hinge (pivot) to the back side. Engage, with extended arms, any free pass rusher that appears within the back side gap. Use shuffling, wide steps as you attempt to drive the defender into a deep arc behind the pocket-depth of the quarterback. If the defending pass rusher goes deep on his own, use your shuffling steps to gain depth with him and thereby, prevent him from crash-rushing the quarterback.

HIT PROTECTION (Quick Passes)

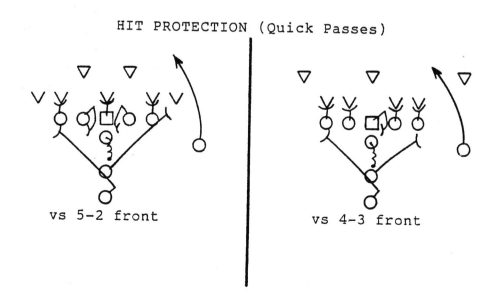

vs 5-2 front   vs 4-3 front

TURNBACK Protection
--play action, pull-up, and roll-out passes--

1. The on side tackle first must <u>identify the defensive tackle</u> and then block him with aggressive HIT blocking techniques. When the offensive tackle is "covered" by a defensive tackle, a quick-strike into his middle will ensue, and followed-up with driving footwork.

    A. During this process, the offensive tackle must keep his feet shoulder-wide and "work" them to gain a position between his defensive opponent and the set-up location of the quarterback.

    B. If the defensive tackle is located to the inside, the on side offensive tackle then will block-down inside and drive his opponent forcefully "to the sideline!"

    C. If three down-linemen are located at the on side (6-2 defense), the on side guard must make a "line call" to his center and tackle and then proceed to block the "covering" opponent with an aggressive HIT block, with the same techniques that are used by his offensive tackle.

        (1) For clarification purposes, a blocking back (full-back) will usually block the defensive end, while the running back (tailback) proceeds to either check-block the on side line-backer, or will release into an opening to run either a "hot" or "hide" route.

2. The back side tackle, back side guard, center, and on side guard (when uncovered) will use a Hinge blocking technique. Each line blocker first must step in unison into their on side gap, bend their knees, and drop their hips while taking a back side hinge (pivot) step.

    A. As these mechanics of technique take place, *each of the hinge blockers should turn in such a way that their legs split the inside leg of their closest blocker.*

    B. Although the objective of each hinge blocker is to keep their buttocks in a line that separates their opponent from the passer, care must be taken <u>not</u> <u>to pivot too much and thereby lose their blocking leverage</u>. Hinge blocking responsibilities follows below...

        (1) ON SIDE GUARD--block the Inside 'A' gap.
        (2) CENTER--block the Back Side 'A' gap.
        (3) BACK SIDE GUARD--block the Back Side 'B' gap.
        (4) BACK SIDE TACKLE--block the Back Side 'C' gap.

C. Each hinge blocker MUST confront ANY opponent that "crosses his face." A hinge blocker has the primary responsibility of extending his arms and the heels of his hands into the chest (jersey numbers) of any crashing, slanting, or looping lineman, or blitzing linebacker, that INTRUDES his territory! Whenever an invader enters this forbidden land, he should be driven outward in an arc as deep as possible.

TURNBACK BLOCKING

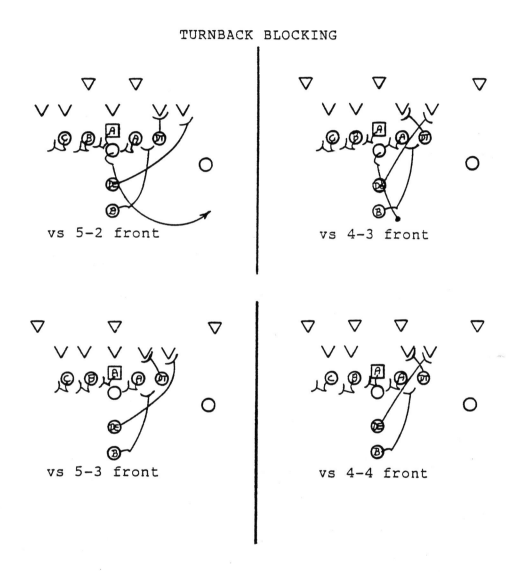

vs 5-2 front

vs 4-3 front

vs 5-3 front

vs 4-4 front

HIT and RECOVER Protection
--3 Step Drop--

1. The pass blocking rules and techniques for the Hit and Recover are identical to that described for Hit protection. The initial explosion of the covered blockers is meant to have the effect of delaying the defensive recognition ("read") of the ensuing pass.

A. As each blocker explodes into his "disruptive strike," they must then disengage immediately from his opponent so that he cannot be pulled, jerked, or slung from his blocking position and/or zone.

B. Any offensive lineman that is uncovered must step first to his inside gap, pivot to his outside and then prepare to "take on" any defender who crosses his face, using controlled, shuffling footwork with arms fully extended and the heels of his hands ready to strike into the shoulder-pad breast plate of the opponent (refer to Turnback Protection techniques).

2. Since this protection is designed for a three-step quarterback drop (pocket), the blockers must take care not to back into the short depth of their quarterback's set-up pocket. If and when blocking contact should be lost, simply apply the age-old standard of "Hit, Recover; Hit, Recover; **Drive!**"

HIT AND RECOVER

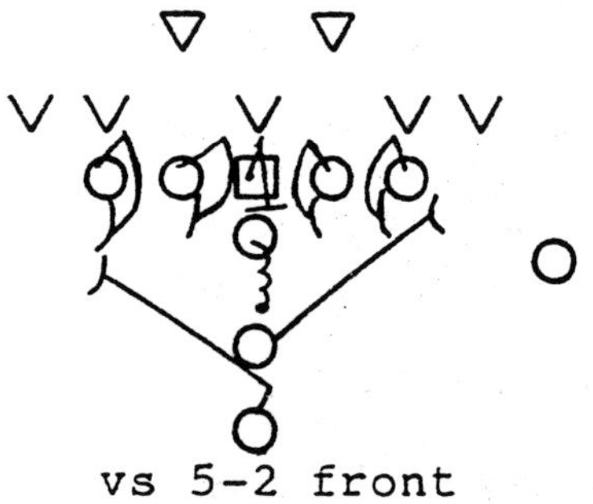

vs 5-2 front

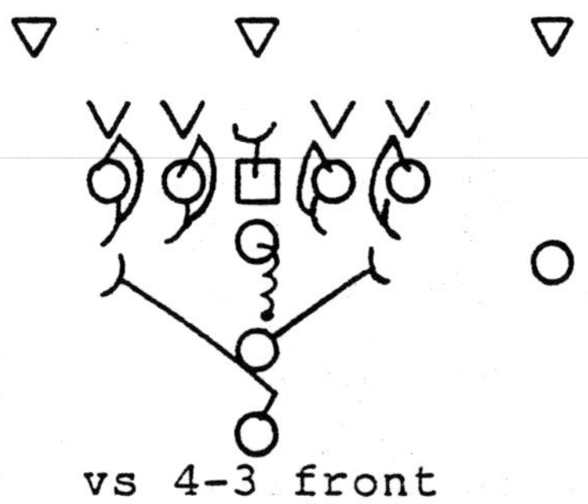

vs 4-3 front

1.   The blocking rules and techniques for the Extend and Hinge have a close relationship to those described for Turnback Protection. The principles of application, however, are symmetrical to both sides of the center. As the football is snapped, the center takes one hop-step backward, while the guards and tackles simultaneously step to their inside with shoulders facing slightly outward. Each blocker now proceeds to crouch his stance, extend his hands, and await the onrush of the defense.

2.   Since the quarterback sets up at a depth of six to seven yards, it is essential that all blocking take place from an inside-to-outside arc.

      A. All challenges made by the defense within the internal gaps must be engaged, since the rushing lanes must be controlled long enough for the quarterback to make his timed pass release.

      B. In a traditional "cup" style of protection, the center first must block any opponent who "covers" him. If a nose guard is not present, the center then is responsible for the entire "middle zone," and thereby will "pick up" the most endangering defensive rusher.

      C. The blocking backs usually block the defensive ends.

3.   An alternative Turn-Out pass-protection method assigns the center to the nose guard or the weak side gap, whichever applies. The guards are assigned to block the first defensive lineman, and the tackles are assigned to block their second defensive lineman.

      A. The blocking backs take responsibility to contain an on side linebacker blitz or defensive end crash.

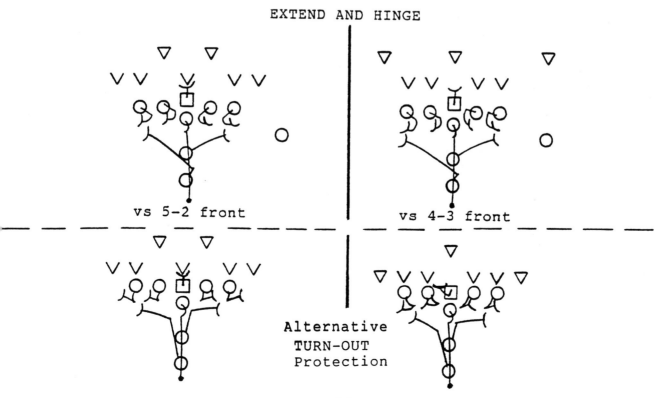

EXTEND AND HINGE

vs 5-2 front   vs 4-3 front

Alternative
TURN-OUT
Protection

RUNNING BACK GUIDELINES

1.   Take an even-footed stance, either two or three-point, depending on the position requirements. Never "telegraph" your play intentions or directions in advance with glancing eyes or a leaning body!

2.   At the start of a play, take your first step always with the on side foot, unless taking an assigned counter or cross-over step.

3.   Concentrate on the attack area, not the ball exchange! The handoff reception should be automatic, from a succession of repetitious practice drills, with the inside elbow held up while the hand faces downward. The opposite (outside) arm and hand should cradle underneath, facing upward. Both hands, resultingly, should cup over the front and rear points of the football.

   A. The shoulders should be squared to the scrimmage line after the ball reception, unless running a "veer course." The football should always be shifted to the outside arm after entering the secondary.

4.   Read the blocking engagements in the attack area and then break for the most accessible opening. Follow your instincts! When pulling or trapping linemen are involved, follow their track before cutting into the intended running lane. On any straight, short-yardage plays, however, follow the initial surge of the blocking linemen to get the first down or touchdown.

5.   Drop your shoulders and conceal chest area when taking part in a play fake. Charge the line as if running with the football, attempting to bait the defense. Try to get tackled, but if this does not happen, you should forge to the second-level as a blocker!

6.   Fold arms softly over the football when designated as the inside runner on any fake-and-give or triple option plays. If the handoff is received, close tightly over the football. On the triple-option, relax the arms whenever the quarterback "pulls" the ball back to his mid section, but continue to run hard as if in possession of the football.

7.   Achieve and maintain a "pitch relationship" with the quarterback on option plays, exactly four yards in depth and four yards in width. Consider this reference as gospel!

8.   Use inside-out leverage when executing a Kick-Out Block against defensive ends, or when carrying out a Fill Block for a pulling lineman.

9.   For wide runs and roll-out passes, approach all Arc Blocks against defensive ends with outside-in leverage.

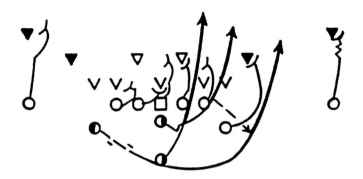

The runner's shoulders should be squared to the line-of-scrimmage, unless running the angled "veer course" (above). The fullback should fold arms softly over the football during the quarterback's hand-off decision. Note the width and depth of four yards for the execution of the option-pitch.

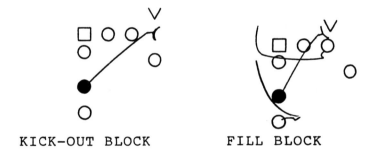

KICK-OUT BLOCK   FILL BLOCK

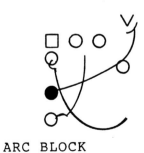

ARC BLOCK

RECEIVER GUIDELINES

1.   Take a two or three-point stance, in compliance with position requirements. Maintain a "poker face" and never tip off an
assignment, either run or pass. Square shoulders to the line-of-
scrimmage.

2.   A wide receiver's stance will usually have a slightly
elongated foot stagger. If the offensive system requires inside
Crack or Shield Blocking, an inside stagger is more efficient and
effective.

3.   Receive all ball-exchanges with inside elbow up with inside
hand facing downward. The opposite arm should cradle underneath,
facing upward. These exchanges can occur from a variiety of mis-
direction-plays.

4.   Give undivided attention to option and reverse-play pitch-
outs! "Look" the football into both hands, giving complete
attention especially to the "final foot" of the football's brief
air flight!

5.   Block defensive backs with an aggressive demeanor! Before
engaging the block, first intimidate the defensive back by pre-
tending to run a pass route, then "run up into his face!"

6.   At the moment of confrontation, explode with an UPLIFTING
WHIP OF THE ARMS, making contact with HEELS OF THE HANDS just
under the defensive back's jersey numbers. Keep hands inside and
"bench press" opponent as your feet take "choppy" steps to
control and deadlock defender.

     A. When Shield Blocking a linebacker to your inside, apply
the fundamentals indicated above. There are two sub categories of
Shield Blocks--the Crack Block and the Screen Block.

     (1) The Crack Block involves taking a direct angle at the
targeted outside linebacker on wide runs toward that side. Prior
to contact, the receiver/blocker "breaks down" into a widened
stance to give allowance for a space cushion, before he begins to
"shadow" the movements of the linebacker. Whenever the linebacker
is frontal to the receiver, a safe and legal block can then be
executed aggressively.

     (2) The Screen Block is specified for the Screen Pass.
The receiver first attempts to "force" run his defensive back
deeper into his coverage area, before retreating into a downward-
to-horizontal arc to wall-off (shield) the outside linebacker.
The receiver's "break down" stance, space cushion, and shadowing
techniques should jointly be applied so that a legal and safe
block can be executed aggressively.

SHIELD BLOCKS

Crack   Screen

(ROUTE/PATTERN SKILLS)

1.   Sprint-release from the scrimmage line without wasted
movements. Make use of your personal speed to apply pressure
vertically on the covering defender.

2.   Strive to develop personal cleverness in footwork techniques
on all routes. Maneuver and experiment with your covering
defenders on play assignments that are far-removed from the
point-of-attack.

3.   Seek "breakdown" opportunities within the deep zone creases
of the opponent's pass coverage, and within the quarterback's
short "scan level" of the curl and hook route zones.

4.   Drive the "covering" defensive back as deep as he will go,
before making the final route break. When the deep-coverage of a
pass defense is "stressed," a "coverage cushion," (space) may
develop between the receiver and his opponent during the final
cut--while the football is airborne.

5.   Attempt always to "jockey" your opponent out of position,
before making the final cut. Drill to acquire timing, consistency, and polish. "Great technique" will result usually from
the drill time that is spent on the fundamental development of
the "little things."

6.   Collect the weight and momentum of your run before making a
sharp route cut. This will necessitate, usually, a "plant" of the
off side foot, which is taken a bit wider than the precluding
steps. Attempt to manipulate an advantageous leverage area in
relationship with the defender. This leverage area is important
in assuring a safe pass reception during the flight of the football.

7.   Advance to the ball while it is airborne! If the ball is
thrown deep, sprint to "get under it."

     A. During the pass reception, relax both hands and cup them
loosely to envelop the incoming ball.

B. Train your eyes to "follow-in" the football, especially during it's "final foot" of flight.

C. Allow hands to "shock absorb" or "give with" the football for a soft, easy-to-manage catch.

D. Clutch football under outside arm immediately after the reception is made! Keep the elbow in a protective "down" position. Your fingers should "wrap around" the front point of the oval-shaped football.

8. Confront "bump-and-run" defensive tactics with (1) Forearm and shoulder uplifts ("Rips"), (2) Footwork pivots off the foot that is either opposite the position of the defender, or to the side of the intended route break, and (3) Head and shoulder fakes and feints that coincide with your evasive movements of the feet.

QUARTERBACK GUIDELINES

1. Assume a stance with bent knees under the center. Be pliable and at ease in composure.

A. Hold your head up and project confidence in appearance and voice. Proceed to take charge of the offense in the huddle and as it breaks for the scrimmage line. Be genuine and personable, but concise, positive, and yet flexible in making decisions. Exert a temperament and voice of command that is in full control!

B. Give a try to the ball exchange technique that eliminates both quarter-turn and sideward wrist movements by the quarterback and center, alike. The techniques follow below...

(1) This method requires the quarterback to hold his thumbs side-by-side, with his palms angled downward and fingers relaxed and spread slightly.

(2) The center, to accommodate the hand placement of the quarterback, must align the tips of the football in a per-pendicular line to that of the scrimmage line (north and south map reference). The football must be snapped straight back to the quarterback, with front point of the ball taking a straight, underneath rotation--which becomes the rear point when the ball exchange is made.

C. Uplift the twin-thumbs pressure under the center to aid him in aiming the football into the ball-exchange area of the quarterback's hands. This pressure also helps promote a forward movement with the center after the snap.

D. Collapse the fingers around the football as it is snapped into the hands. As the ball is secured, advance it immediately to belt-line area.

2. Examine both sides of the line in the same mode of consistency on every play! A good poker player will take care to avoid tipping-off the hand to be played, and a good field general must take care to do the same before vocalizing his cadence.

3. Use your eyes to follow all hand offs--or fake hand offs-- made to any of your running backs. When executing a fake exchange, be certain to keep your "body language" the same as that displayed during an actual hand off.

4. All hand offs must be placed firmly into the stomach of the intended ball carrier. All fake exchanges should be performed either as a jab fake or ride fake with a "light touch" before withdrawl. The ride fake uses a flow with the arms while the football is placed deceptively into the midsection of his play-acting running back.

5. Practice footwork techniques on a daily basis. Practice is necessary to improve and remain sharp. Even the professionals have to maintain their practice rituals and regimens, which is intensified by the pressure to perform on a level that is greater than someone of a "lesser league." The two basic quarterback footwork methods will follow next...

   A. Direct Step Method: A straight line approach to the hand off area. The quarterback's initial step is taken with his near side foot. This method is often used for quick-striking hand offs, straight traps and, oftentimes, on sprint-draw plays.

   B. Pivot (Spin) Step Method: Involves a spin-out exit from the center. The quarterback's initial pivot takes place off his on side foot. The approach to the hand off area is customarily deep because the usual purpose of the Pivot (Spin) Step Method is to (1) Conceal the football from the defense, and (2) Allow the running back who receives the exchange to have a desirable backfield depth to make perceptual cuts for the "daylight" openings along the scrimmage line.

6. When executing a keep-or-pitch option play, attack the inside shoulder of the defensive end. The general guideline for the quarterback on option plays is to manipulate the defense within the off-tackle running lane on the "keeper," and thus leave the advantageous wide flank to the option-pitch runner.

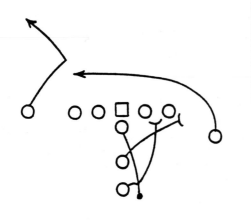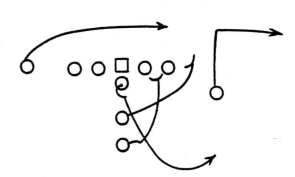

Direct (Open) Step Method
w/timed In & Out (Post-
Corner) route break.

Pivot (Spin) Step Method
w/timed Out route break.

(PASSING TIDBITS)

1. Develop the five basic steps of a pass delivery! Their identity and explanation will follow below...

   A. Collection, Grip and Carry: Remember first to place upward pressure under the center with twin-thumbs prior to the ball snap to give the center his ball-exchange aim and also to help promote a forward movement with the center after the snap.

   (1) Collect the ball-snap from the center quickly and securely into the belt-line area before attempting to step away from the scrimmage line. Avoid the pitfall of "leaving the ball behind" (fumble) because of an over-anxiousness to make a convincing play fake or to set up quickly into the intended depth of the pass protection pocket.

   (2) Grip the football where the little finger makes contact with the center of the lace. Hold the palm over the ball with a little air space in between, taking care not to apply a "choke hold." The index finger should be placed slightly to the rear of the ball, depending upon the size of the hand, so that a desirable nose-up ball release can be attained. The free hand should be placed along the other side of the football for both stability and security.

   (3) Carry the football with the protection of both hands during the running approach to the set-up pocket or roll-out passing zone. Grip and guard the ball just to the left or right side of the chest, in a "ready position," for a quick and natural pass release.

   B. Pocket Set Up: May be executed either with a Direct Step Method or a Pivot (Spin) Step Method as the quarterback makes an exit from center. Get the necessary depth from the line as quickly as possible. The footwork mechanics involved in setting up in the pocket behind the on side guard are...

(1) A quick-stop braking action with the outside foot must be taken to bring the body's inertia to a controlled draw-up.

        (a) A right-handed quarterback, therefore, would collect-up on his right foot when setting up behind the right guard, with his shoulders aligned perpendicular to the scrimmage line.

        (b) When setting up behind the left guard, a right-handed quarterback would collect-up on his left foot, then "Hop-Around" onto his right foot, and align his shoulders with the identical perpendicular relationship to the scrimmage line as used when setting up on the right side.

(2) A lead-off step with the target foot (foot opposite the throwing arm) must be taken in the direction of the target area or receiver.

    C. **Timing Factor and Read**: May be executed from the traditional <u>Yard-Depth Route Break</u> or the unique Time-beat Route Break that was developed in the 1970's and used successfully by Coach Frank Kush of Arizona State University. An explanation of the two quarterback-receiver methods of reading and coordinating the precision factors of accurate passing follows below...

    (1) <u>Yard-Depth Route Break</u>--A predesigned structure of individual pass routes or multiple-receiver patterns in which there is a limit to the number of yards that each receiver will run up-the-field or diagonally before making the critical cut to "break open" for the airborne pass. Much depends on defensive alignments and coverages--receivers have to adjust speed and timing based on variable coverages. Both receiver and quarterback must have coordination in reading these keys.

    (2) Time-Beat Route Break--A preset timing factor of seconds that can determine when the receivers make their final cut in conjunction with the quarterback's timed pass release of the football.

    (a) The <u>military march beat</u> is the timing factor that is emphasized here. The exact tempo can be measured, monitored, and controlled with preciseness by a metronome and, also, by hand claps in unison during practice sessions, although with slightly less exactness.

    (b) This exact-tempo concept enhances the individual speed and abilities of the receivers, conversely, by <u>not</u> restricting a receiver's speed and attributes by placing a limitation on the depth of his personal footwork cuts and routes. The advantage herein is that a fast receiver is not inadvertently placed on the same level as a slow receiver. Tight defensive coverages can be *stretched* vertically with true efficiency when all receivers can be "let loose" to explore their natural running speed--containing the threat of the deep "bomb" is realistically *forced* upon the defensive backs, while the linebackers will experience that their coverage box (zone) has taken deeper proportions.

(c) Certain circumstances, it should be noted, will require controlled routes when attempting to pass in various down-and-distance and goal-line situations.

(d) This "fire it now" principle applies to the quarterback's "primary read!" The usual factors for route depth will follow below...

- Quick Passes are set, generally, for a PASS RELEASE TIMED for TWO or THREE STEPS.

- Play Action, and Pocket Passes (6 to 7 yards) are set for a RELEASE TIMED for SEVEN to TWELVE ROUTE STEPS.

- Roll-Out Passes are often set for a receiver group that is running FIVE, TEN, and FIFTEEN YARD ROUTE STEPS! The pass release factor for a roll-out pass has pathway timing variations. This is because the quarterback usually will have more time to "throw on his own instinct," whereas typical pocket passes will necessitate a release at a given time, due to line blocking and linebacker recovery considerations.

- When throwing from a structured pocket behind the on side guard, in contrast, the quarterback is required to "pull up" a full count sooner so that his pass can be released "on time"--at the start of the receiver's route breaks.

- Whenever the quarterback rejects the receiver choices in his primary read, he then must turn to his second-choice read and prepare to "fire" or "dump" the football to an open receiver in that group.

- The individual receivers should be instructed to make their deceptive head and shoulder movements before attempting to separate from their defender.

D. Release: Begins with a smooth, pre-release movement of the football from the high-chest area to a position just to the rear of the ear lobe before transferring the energy of motion into a forward thrust. Prior to the forward movement of the pass release, both hands still should be on the football, with the bent elbow pointing to the rear and held level to the ground.

- As the forward throwing movement begins, the foot opposite the throwing arm must be planted precisely at the contemplated target. When the ball begins to zip past the ear, the elbow should be slightly in front. Be aware that the actual strength of the pass and the quickness of its release are more dependent on the rotation of the upper body than on the strength

of the arm! As the ball is released, the thumb of the throwing
hand should point <u>downward</u> to assure a proper lock of the wrist
and a correct release of the football from the tip of the index
finger.

- Whether or not the flight of the football will
be released in an arc or in a straight projectile will be
determined primarily by WHEN the ball is "let go." A high-
shoulder release will tend to yield an arcing ball in flight,
whereas a pass released from chin level will tend to take the
form of a straight "bullet" pass. The quarterback should always
"roll his weight" onto his front leg to assure a firm throw.
During this shift of weight from the back foot to the front
(lead) foot, therefore, be sure to engage the pushing force of
the rear leg and hips during the pass release.

E. Follow-up: Begins with the passer's arm swing that is <u>in
line with the alignment of his spinal column</u>. This arm-whip
movement takes place in time with a plant of the lead step.
Cross-body throws should not occur if care is taken to coordinate
(1) Your set-up of the feet and shoulders in conjunction with
your upper-body rotation, (2) A well-aligned plant (lead) step,
(3) A straight arm whip of the ball, and (4) A release of the
football from the tip of your index finger.

2. Display Poise When Under Competitive Pressure!

A. Be oblivious to the pass-rush pressure and focus your
complete attention to the secondary coverage keys--and to the
maneuvering of your pass receivers.

B. If the primary choice is discounted, maintain composure
and scan the perimeter for an outlet or second-receiver choice.

C. In order to maintain composure, remember that personal
discipline must be maintained! Throw on the timing of the route
breaks within the pass pattern. Do not risk an interception by
waiting for a receiver to get extra steps on his defender before
releasing the football.

3. Develop Trajectory Levels to Match the Depth and Breaking
Angle of all Designed Routes! The flight levels that suit the
route types, in general, are recommended below...

A. Straight (bullet) Ball--used generally on routes directed
through the underneath (linebacker) zones and, also, on break-out
routes into the flats. The football usually is thrown from the
head-to-shoulder level of the receivers with this type of pass
trajectory.

B. Air Ball--used on most deep routes, inside and outside, whenever an arc is prudent in passing the ball safely to a long-range receiver. With this type of trajectory, the targeted receiver should "run to" the reception point. Passes thrown into the underneath zone must be firm, but sometimes will need a "drop-down" arc if the linebackers arm reach tend to present a potential risk.

C. Dump Ball--used primarily on quick-release passes and screen passes. The crispness of the release usually is determined by (1) The distance of the intended receiver, and (2) The presence and the calibre of both the linebackers and defensive backs.

PASS TRAJECTORY LEVELS

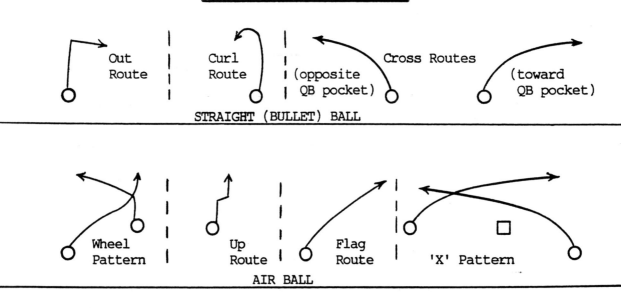

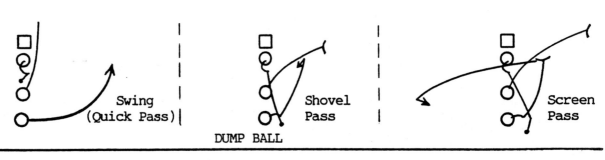

NUMERICAL MATCHUPS WHEN FACING DOUBLE-COVERAGES

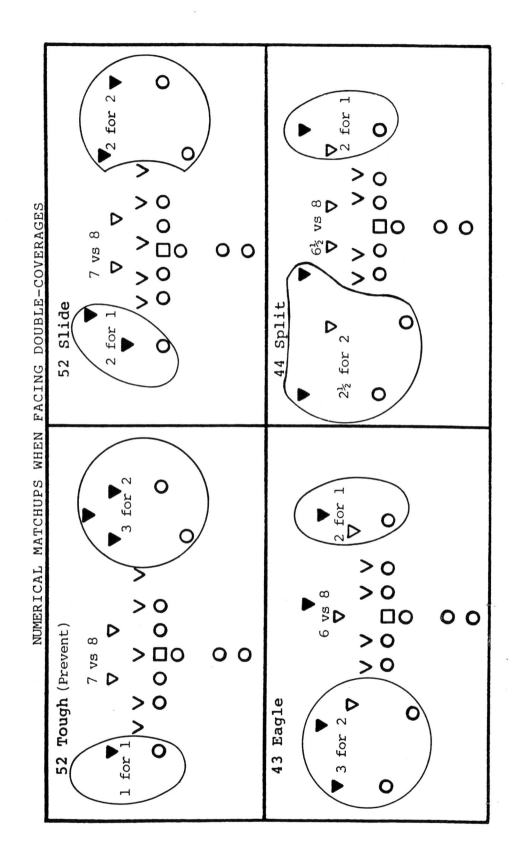

HYPOTHETICAL "HOLES" IN ZONE COVERAGES

These vulnerable areas can be explored best if
linebackers are held-up and secondary rotations
are "frozen" with play-action fake in the backfield. Combination coverages will tend to eliminate "obvious" zone holes, but new weaknesses
will open-up when secondary is forced to cover
two receivers within attack area (the quarterback's first option read).

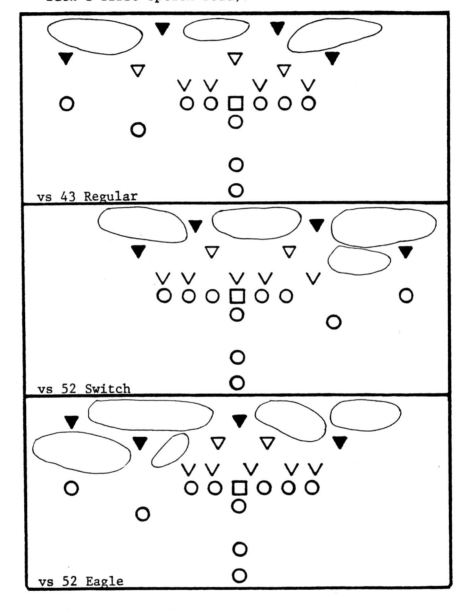

vs 43 Regular

vs 52 Switch

vs 52 Eagle

IV

BLENDING OLDER CONCEPTS WITH THE FAMILIAR

Use of Overload Formations

The **Overload Sets** use an offensive concept that embodies the elements of the Flexbone-T/Spread/Run-and-Shoot and the Offset-I offensive systems with those of the classic Unbalanced-Line Double Wing-T from the 1940's, 1950's, and early 1960's. This blend is accomplished by using both Double Slot and Offset-I backfield alignments with one of the ends aligned inside the split end of the "overload side," or by designating another lineman to position himself as a "twin tackle" to the unbalanced side. With this twin tackle arrangement, the end man on the Short Side (the short end) is eligible as a pass receiver if he is wearing a receiver's jersey number. Even if the end man on the Short Side is wearing a lineman's jersey number (when the flex end "overloads" to the opposite side), he will continue to function as a blocker and the defense must recognize and contain the threat of an unbalanced-line side and a short-flank side. Some of the broad advantages of this offensive plan are:

(1) A balanced format of running plays maintains its presence due to the varying usage of (A) Two-step deep motion, (B) Comeback motion, and (C) Horizontal motion, from one of the slot backs, or from (D) Flash motion by the fullback when he is offset (illustrated below). These innovations must be a basic part of the style of play if an "overload" concept is embraced!

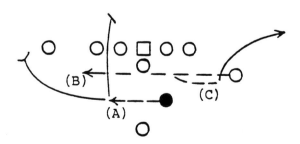

(A) Illustrates Flash Motion by the fullback from an Offset alignment to balance the lead-blocker segment of a play format. (B) Illustrates horizontal Motion by the slot back to alter the strength of the alignment. (C) Illustrates Comeback Motion by the slot back to either balance or "check-balance" the play format.

(2) The Overloaded (end over) Side will either (A) Bring about an equal matching of defensive strength against offensive strength, or (B) Influence a rotatation of the opponent's

secondary to the strength of the formation, or (C) Influence an overcompensating defensive adjustment to the unbalanced side, or, lastly, (D) Attain blocking leverage or pass route/pattern advantages if and when the opposition fails to make adequate adjustments to the Overloaded Side. A miscalculation in adjustment to either side can result in containment breakdowns!

(3) The Overloaded Side retains its reliable slot back/ split end passing attack. An extra blocker, the end that's "overloaded," is invaluable in giving blocking enforcement to that side, especially in goal-line and short-yardage situations.

(4) The availability of eligible receivers on the Short Side will depend, naturally, on the specific alignment that is dispersed. The practical maximum is three receivers, namely the eligible short end, the on side slot back, a back in motion, and a flashing fullback or slot back who makes a cross from the short side to the unbalanced-line side.

> Various combinations from basic Wishbone-T, Wing-T, and Slot-I attacks are evident within the play structures of the Overload concept. The primary assault plan described below include ingredients that are embraced by many coaches as the foundational building blocks of winning football:

(1) The Inside Veer Option, the Midline Option, the Counter Reverse, the Counter Trey, the middle Trap, the Trap Option, the Wham, the Wham Keep, the Speed Option, and the off-tackle Sweep, with its companion Bootleg, are all solid and reliable plays that have great potency to their designated sides.

(2) A concise exploitation of the Short and Overload Sides can take place both in the running and passing attacks. The opposing defenses are compelled to make choices in covering the short and long flanks, to contain the run and to provide adequate support in its coverage of potential pass receivers. When any receiver draws a man-on-man coverage, perhaps the Run-and-Shoot principle of testing skill-against-skill can be probed. The Overload sets place a similar stress upon opposing defenses, such as those demonstrated by the Air Force Academy's Flexible-T offense in the late 1950's and early 1960's.

> This grass-roots assortment of proven offensive plays is a surviving part of the heritage of American football. Blocking assignments are relatively easy to apply. The variety and deception of the plays should be more than adequate, as well.

+ + + + + + +

★ The prime requisite of a successful **overload offensive plan**, however, is the availability of a durable, quick-footed, and competitive runner to perform faithfully at the running-back position! All player positions certainly are important in every offensive system, but it should be restated that the Double Slot and Offset-I alignments, especially, will require credible performers at both the quarterback and deep running-back posi- tions if any realistic offensive advantages are to be gained.

(1) The OVERLOAD-I: This "end over" set combines the advantages of the Overload Flexbone and Offset-I into an alignment with unbalanced strength. All eligible receivers have the advantage of congestion-free releases from the line on pass routes/patterns. If an opponent's defense can be caught in momentary confusion, or if the opposition makes an overcompensating adjustment to the unbalanced strength of the formation, a game-winning "break" may occur. Since the flexed end is aligned as an outside tackle on the unbalanced side, he is *not* an eligible receiver. His split alignment, however, forces a wide outside containment that positions him as a valuable blocker in the defensive secondary, which serves also in stretching the coverage of the opposing secondary. This "stretched alignment" is particularly effective against "attack defenses" by forcing them out of their ganged-up stacks within the middle. A use of Flash Motion by the fullback is helpful also in diversifying the formation's Short Side potentiality to an even-greater extent. If league rules should disallow the use of an ineligible-receiver number on the end of the line, personnel exchanges would become a necessity.

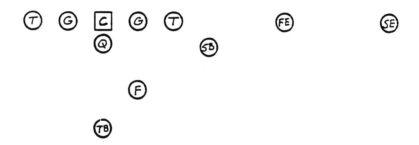

(2) The OVERSET-I w/twin tackles: The philosophical objective is to form a tight coupling of Unbalanced Single Wing, Wing-T and Offset-I principles of attack. This design is meant to provide a concentration of running and passing potentialities to the unbalanced side, and option and reverse-play opportunities to the least-manned (short) side.

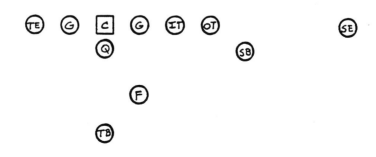

(3) The FLEX WINGBONE: This tight end/wingback adaptation adds
"muscle" to the short side of the field, without losing the ver-
satility of a four-receiver Flexbone style of attack. Although
this balanced alignment does not qualify as an unbalanced-
receiver set, its presence in the structure serves as a prelude
to its companion Overload Flexbone formation (portrayed next).

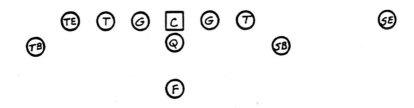

(4) The OVERLOAD FLEXBONE: This alignment presents rotational
problems to the opponent's secondary in its quest to defend the
passing attack to the overload side and, also, the bilateral
option attack. This set serves well, especially, as a tactical
change-up. A slow recognition and adjustment response by the
defense could result in timely gains, both in running and
passing. If league rules should disallow the use of an ineligible-receiver
number on the end of the line, personnel exchanges would become a necessity.

OVERLOAD-I

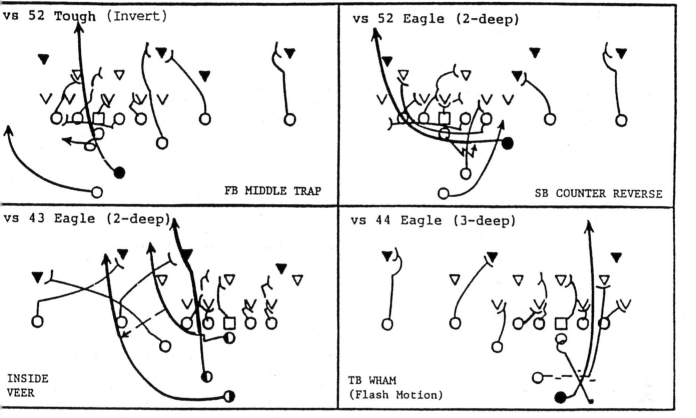

vs 52 Tough (Invert)

FB MIDDLE TRAP

vs 52 Eagle (2-deep)

SB COUNTER REVERSE

vs 43 Eagle (2-deep)

INSIDE
VEER

vs 44 Eagle (3-deep)

TB WHAM
(Flash Motion)

PLAY ASSIGNMENTS FOR OVERLOAD-I:

Diagram 1: FULLBACK MIDDLE TRAP

Blocking Scheme: PST--block inside linebacker; PSG--down-block inside/if N/A, exit-block to outside; Center--block man over or back side; BSG--pull and trap defensive tackle; BST--scoop the down lineman zone (DLZ).

Fulfillments: The quarterback begins with a direct, open step from center to weak side at a yard's depth, as if pitching the ball. He then pivots inside for hand off to off-set fullback at the onside hip of center, completes spin, and continues down line.

Diagram 3: INSIDE VEER

Blocking Scheme (Zone): PSWR--block the nearest safety; Overload End--block the free safety; PSSB--arc release and block corner back; PST--block inside linebacker; PSG--block #1 defender; Center--block the play side track; BSG & BST--block the DLZ.

Fulfillments: The quarterback open-steps to play side, reaches-back with arms and near foot, and greets full-back with ball at waist level behind the on side guard while scanning the "read key" outside tackle. The "give" is made unless read key attacks--then ball is withdrawn and keep-or-pitch option is read versus pitch key/EMOL.

Diagram 2: SB COUNTER REVERSE

Blocking Scheme: PST--down-block to the inside; PSG--down-block inside; (may combo block w/center) Center--block over/fill the back side A-gap; BSG--pull and trap far side EMOL; BST--pull and lead block; Overload End--Block pitch support (OLB/SS).

Fulfillments: The quarterback begins with a deep open step from center to belly-ride ball with fullback, then takes an additional step backward to make a forward hand off to slot back as he runs a timed course toward the far side C-gap (trap zone).

Diagram 4: TB WHAM (FLASH MOTION)

Blocking Scheme: PST--block #2 on the line-of-scrimmage (LOS); PSG--block #1 on LOS; Center--block play side track (gap to 2nd level); BSG, BST & BSSB--block DLZ (BSG may also "combo block" with BST versus 43 defensive front); Overload End--block free safety; Fullback--"flash," then wham (drive) block the on side linebacker.

Fulfillments: The quarterback reverse-spins from center to make his hand off to tailback 3-4 yards in the backfield, then sets up behind the on side guard at a seven-yard depth. The tailback must read fullback's block.

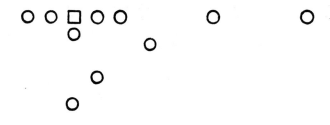

OVERSET-I w/ twin tackles

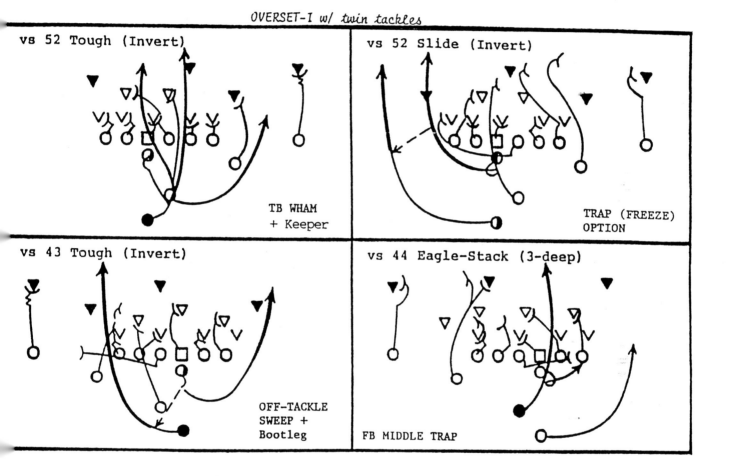

vs 52 Tough (Invert)

TB WHAM
+ Keeper

vs 52 Slide (Invert)

TRAP (FREEZE)
OPTION

vs 43 Tough (Invert)

OFF-TACKLE
SWEEP +
Bootleg

vs 44 Eagle-Stack (3-deep)

FB MIDDLE TRAP

PLAY ASSIGNMENTS FOR OVERSET-I w/TWIN TACKLES:

Diagram 1: TAILBACK WHAM + KEEPER

Blocking Scheme (Tight Side): PSSB--block pitch support; PSOT--load block end man on line (EMOL); PSIT & PSG--block the down-lineman over or inside (if uncovered, block/double-team to inside); Center--block over or play side gap; BSG & BSE--block the DLZ; Fullback--wham (drive) block the ILB.

Fulfillments: The quarterback reverse-spins from center to make a quick-ride hand off (or keeper fake) at a 3-4 yard depth in the backfield. On the keeper, he first must make a convincing ride-fake before turning up field to maneuver for goal line.

Diagram 3: OFF-TACKLE SWEEP + BOOTLEG

Blocking Scheme (G-pull): PSSE--force block the corner back; PSSB--block inside; PSOT--block EMOL; PSIT--block down lineman over or inside; PSG--pull to play side and block EMOL; Center--block play side track; BSG--scoop block the DLZ; BSE--rake and release (R & R); Fullback--fill the on side B-gap for pulling guard.

Fulfillments: The tailback receives toss from quarterback on a downhill course, looks for a defensive soft spot, and explodes into opening. A quarterback Bootleg may be included.

Diagram 2: TRAP (FREEZE) OPTION

Blocking Scheme: PSE--block inside linebacker; PSG--block down lineman over or inside; Center--block over or back side; BSG--pull and log block defender aligned over the short side end; BSIT--block the DLZ; BSOT--R & R; BSSB--clear deep crease.

Fulfillments: Open pivot, step backward behind center at a yard's depth, and fake hand off to fullback. Pause, then drive down the short-side line and read the pitch key to determine whether to keep or option pitch the football to tailback.

Diagram 4: FULLBACK MIDDLE TRAP

Blocking Scheme: PSE--block inside linebacker; PSG--block the inside lineman or linebacker (if N/T, exit-block to outside); Center--block man over or back side; BSG--pull and trap block defensive tackle; BSIT--block the DLZ to 2nd level; BSOT--R & R.

Fulfillments: The quarterback begins with a direct, open step from center to weak side at a yard's depth, as if pitching the ball. An inside pivot then is made for the hand off to off-set fullback at onside hip of center. A Trap Option fake by the quarterback completes the play.

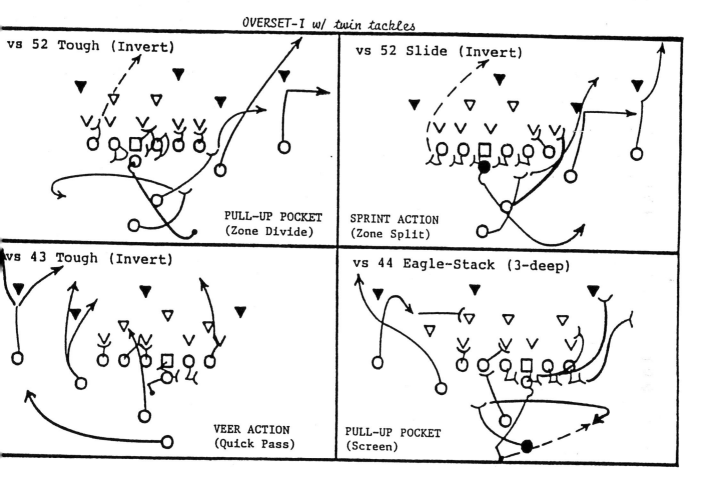

OVERSET-I w/ twin tackles

vs 52 Tough (Invert)

PULL-UP POCKET
(Zone Divide)

vs 52 Slide (Invert)

SPRINT ACTION
(Zone Split)

vs 43 Tough (Invert)

VEER ACTION
(Quick Pass)

vs 44 Eagle-Stack (3-deep)

PULL-UP POCKET
(Screen)

Pass Blocking Schemes and Synopsis of Patterns

Diagram 5 Protection Scheme: Aggressive Hit & Recover pass protection techniques (Chapter II) apply for the play side outside and inside tackles, the strong guard, and the center against the down-linemen in their outside-to-inside area of responsibility.

When uncovered, the aforementioned linemen will take their initial step into their on side gaps, pivot, and then apply cup protection techniques to their back side.

The back side Short Guard will step inside, pivot, and then cup protect whether covered or uncovered.

Synopsis: The Zone *Divide* pattern combines the strong side split end's Out route with his companion slot back's straight-line Flag route.

Split End--run an Out route, which consists of a sharp 45 degree break toward the sideline. When executing the break, the body weight should be brought under control prior to the outside cut, first by widening his steps, and then by planting his inside foot--in conjunction with an inside head feint--before pushing-off forcefully to the outside. A snap of the elbows to the outside will help to sharpen the shift of weight to the outside. Know always the location of the sideline so that <u>one foot</u>, at least, will be planted in bounds during a pass reception.

Slot back--run a Flag route, which is merely a straight-line drive for the goal line flag, and expect the flight of the ball between the body and the sideline; Quarterback--roll-out toward the Strong Side, while reading the defensive commitment of the corner back. A pass release to the slot back should have "air" under it's trajectory, with a slight lead given. A pass release to the split end should have a sharp, low driving trajectory with the ball placed between the sideline and receiver, at chest level.

Short End--rake the outside defender and release into a deep Crease route over the middle from the back side, splitting two defensive backs. Expect the quarterback's pass release to develop from his own timing.

The fullback will check the EMOL and engage him if not blocked by the outside tackle (if clear, release into the flat at a 5-yard depth as a flood receiver).

The tailback first will check for a B-gap blitz, then fake a screen-pass release and stand by as an outlet receiver.

- -

Diagram 6 Protection Scheme: Apply a modified Turnback Protection blocking scheme.

The outside tackle determines the location of the defensive tackle and blocks him aggressively with Run blocking techniques.

The inside tackle and all other lineman are instructed to pivot to their back side gaps at a 35 degree angle, thereby splitting the outside leg of their innermost blocking lineman and, thereby, prepare to aggressively engage any defender who crosses in front of their face (zone). Thus, the areas of blocking accountability for the remaining linemen will fall into the following order:

(1) Inside Tackle--B-gap, (2) Strong Guard--A-gap, (3) Center--back side A-gap, (4) Short Guard--back side B-gap, and (5) Short End--back side C-gap, which is followed by a delayed release as a back side receiver, whenever practicable.

The fullback will arc block the end man on the line (EMOL).

The tailback will check for a B-gap blitz, then release through the scrimmage area to run a 10-yard Fan route.

Synopsis: The Zone *Split* pattern combines the Strong Side split end's Up route with his companion slot back's Out route. The split end's Up (fade) route consists of a 35 degree cut to the outside (inside foot plant), then another cut taken up the sideline on the third step (outside foot plant).

The slot back's Out route consists of a sharp 45 degree break toward the sideline. When executing the break, his body weight should be brought under control prior to his outside cut, first by widening his steps, and then by planting his inside foot--in conjunction with an inside head feint--before pushing-off forcefully to the outside. A snap of the elbows to the outside helps to sharpen his shift of weight to the outside.

The quarterback should roll-out toward the Strong Side, and then read the defensive commitment of the corner back. The football's pass trajectory to the split end should have "air" under it, with a slight lead, but a pass made to the slot back during his Out route should have a sharp, low driving trajectory at chest level.

The wingback runs a deep crease route over the middle from the back side, splitting two defensive backs, and should expect a pass thrown to him to occur from the quarterback's own timing process.

- -

Diagram 7 Protection Scheme: Aggressive Hit & Recover pass protection techniques (Chapter II) apply for the play side side outside and inside tackles, the strong guard, and the center against the down-linemen in their outside-to-inside area of responsibility.

When uncovered, an aforementioned linemen will will usually block to his inside to render aid to his inside blocker against a stubborn down lineman, but he can block to his outside to render blocking aid when needed.

The short guard will apply cup protection techniques to his back side, as will the center if he is uncovered.

The short end should rake and release (R & R) into his pass route. The fullback will fake a veer play exchange and block the on side linebacker.

Synopsis: The *Quick Pass* is the simpliest pass-play innovation of all time, which completes the fourth dimension to the veer (triple) option play.

Quarterback--ride/jab fake with fullback, take one step to the rear, read the seams that the receivers are slicing, and quick-fire the football.

Slot Back--although illustrated in a blocking role, he can release easily between the inside linebacker and strong safety to begin a slant-in route.

Split End--should first read the coverage depth of the defensive backs, then run a quick slant-in route between the corner back and strong safety;

Short End--run the back side crease between the corner back and outside linebacker or safety.

The tailback will swing to the play side on an option-pitch course, as an outlet receiver.

- -

Diagram 8 Protection Scheme: The illustrated blocking scheme for the Short Side *Screen* pass is established from Turnback Protection guidelines.

Short End--begin play with a Hinge Block for 3 seconds, release outside to establish the screen wall, then block the corner support on the "BALL" command from the tailback.

Short Guard--use a Hinge Block for 3 seconds, release to the outside, establish a 4-5 feet distance inside the short end, and then Lead Block up the field on the "BALL" command from the tailback.

Center--use a Hinge Block for 3 seconds, release to side of screen wall and seal the critical area inside the short side guard, and then surge up the field on tailback's "BALL" command.

Strong Guard, and Inside and Outside Tackle--apply and maintain Turnback Protection principles.

Fullback--zone block the area between the B and C-gaps.

Synopsis: The Short Side *Screen* pass begins from the quarterback's pull-up pocket at the formation's Strong Side. This pass call should be reserved at such a time when the defense is either over shifted to the strong side, or over playing to that side in some way.

Quarterback--set up behind the strong guard, bait the defense into a false "key" recognition by looking up the field during the silent 3-second delayed count, then turn toward the Short Side flank to release the pass softly to the tailback.

Tailback--before receiving the screen pass, first pretend to protect the B-gap in support for the fullback, but "lose" whatever blocking contact that may be encountered with an opponent. Then slip to the Short Side, behind the scrimmage line, and set up for the pass at a 2-yard depth and a 4-yard distance from the short end's original position. After receiving the pass, "tuck" the ball in outside arm, give "BALL" command to line blockers, and then follow behind blocking surge of the screen-wall blockers!

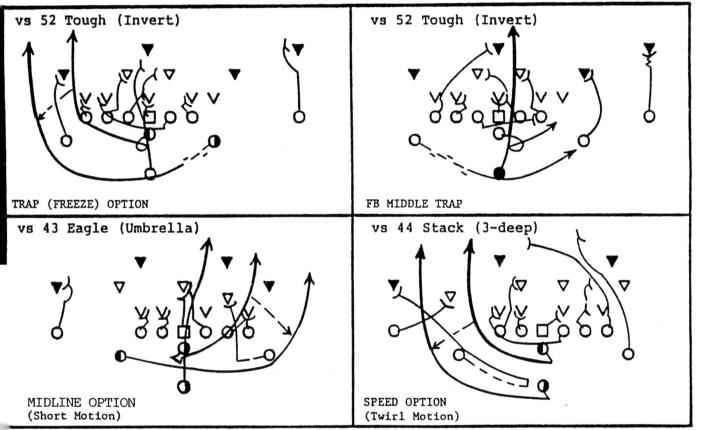

vs 52 Tough (Invert)

TRAP (FREEZE) OPTION

vs 52 Tough (Invert)

FB MIDDLE TRAP

vs 43 Eagle (Umbrella)

MIDLINE OPTION
(Short Motion)

vs 44 Stack (3-deep)

SPEED OPTION
(Twirl Motion)

PLAY ASSIGNMENTS FOR FLEX WINGBONE:

Diagram 1: TRAP (FREEZE) OPTION

Blocking Scheme: PSWB--arc release to block the pitch support; PSTE--load block end man on line (EMOL); PST--block inside linebacker; PSG--block down lineman aligned over or inside; Center--block over or back side; BSG--pull and log block the defensive tackle; BST--scoop block the DLZ.

Fulfillments: The quarterback begins with an open step from center at yard's depth, completes inside pivot and fakes a hand off to fullback at on side hip of center. Then he runs outside EMOL to keep or lateral to slot back from reaction to secondary.

Diagram 3: MIDLINE OPTION (SHORT MOTION)

Blocking Scheme: PSWB--use short motion, then wham block inside linebacker; PSTE--load block EMOL; PST--block outside to isolate defensive tackle; PSG--block inside; Center--block opponent over or back side; BSG and BST--scoop block the DLZ.

Fulfillments: The quarterback begins with a drop step to back side A-gap, reads the defensive tackle (read key) as fullback strikes over center at midline. If read key pinches, the quarterback keeps inside or option pitches off the outside contain man.

Diagram 2: FULLBACK MIDDLE TRAP

Blocking Scheme: PSSB--arc block the pitch suport; PST--block inside linebacker; PSG--down-block to inside/if N/T, exit-block to outside; Center--block over or back side; BSG--pull and trap defensive tackle; BST--scoop block the DLZ.

Fulfillments: The quarterback begins with a direct, open step from center to weak side at a yard's depth, makes an inside pivot and hands off ball to fullback at the onside hip of center. Then he completes the spin, and continues down line for option fake.

Diagram 4: SPEED OPTION (TWIRL MOTION)

Blocking Scheme: PSSE--crack block inside; PSSB--use twirl motion, then block corner back; PST--block inside linebacker; PSG--block the down lineman over or inside; Center--block the down lineman over or back side (fill); BSG--pull and log block read key; BST--rake and release (R & R).

Fulfillments: The quarterback and the fullback begin 2-way option with a drop-step toward back side to allow time for defense to commit to a false play flow. This occurs during slot back's twirl motion, which sets up the log block by the back side guard.

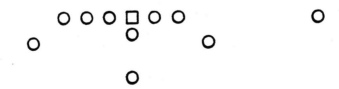

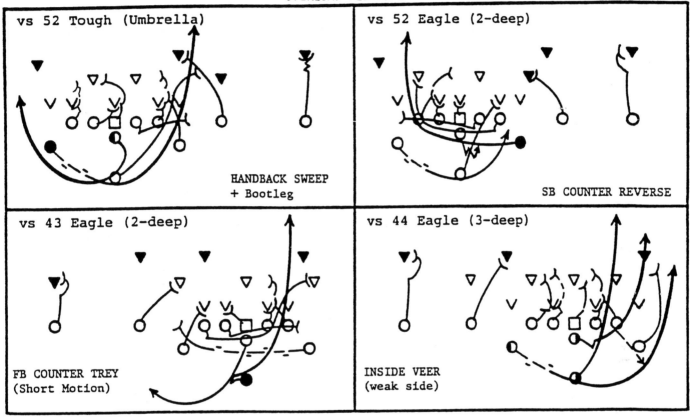

vs 52 Tough (Umbrella)

HANDBACK SWEEP
+ Bootleg

vs 52 Eagle (2-deep)

SB COUNTER REVERSE

vs 43 Eagle (2-deep)

FB COUNTER TREY
(Short Motion)

vs 44 Eagle (3-deep)

INSIDE VEER
(weak side)

PLAY ASSIGNMENTS FOR OVERLOAD FLEXBONE:

Diagram 1: HANDBACK SWEEP + BOOTLEG

Blocking Scheme: Split End--force block corner back; Flex End--block the deep safety; PSSB--block inside; PST--block the down lineman aligned over or inside; PSG--pull to the play side and trap block end man on line (EMOL); Center--block the play side track; BSG--block the DLZ; BST--rake and release (R & R).

Fulfillments: The quarterback open steps play side at a 3-4 yard midline depth for hand off to the wingback in motion, then fakes or runs a Bootleg. Ball carrier arc-runs through C-gap.

Diagram 3: FB COUNTER TREY (SHORT MOTION)

Blocking Scheme: PST--down-block or combo block with PSG (blocker with least pressure bounces to the middle/ far side linebacker); PSG--down-block or combo with PST; Center--fill back side A-gap; BSG--pull and trap block the far side EMOL; BST--pull and lead block through play side C-gap for runner; BSSB--block inside to seal.

Fulfillments: The quarterback open steps from center to back side in the guise of a roll-out pass, while the fullback takes a slide step, a cross-over step, and an adjustment step to the back side to receive the ball.

Diagram 2: SLOT BACK COUNTER REVERSE

Blocking Scheme: PST--down-block or combo block with PSG (blocker with least pressure bounces to the middle/ far side linebacker); PSG--block down lineman over or inside; Center--fill back side A-gap; BSG--pull and trap block far side EMOL; BST--pull and lead block through play side C-gap.

Fulfillments: The quarterback open-steps to play side, reaches-back with arms and near foot to greet fullback with ball at waist level behind back side guard for fake hand off. Then he takes a step backward and makes a frontal hand off to the on side slot back as he dashes for far side C-gap.

Diagram 4: INSIDE VEER (weak side)

Blocking Scheme: PSWB--arc release and block pitch support; PST--block inside linebacker; PSG--block the #1 defender; Center--block the play side track; BSG--block the DLZ; BST--R & R.

Fulfillments: The quarterback open-steps to play side, reaches-back with arms and near foot, and greets full-back with ball at waist level behind on side guard, while viewing "read key" outside tackle. The "give" is made unless read key attacks--then ball is withdrawn for outside option.

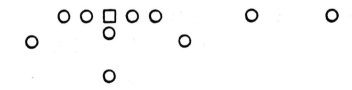

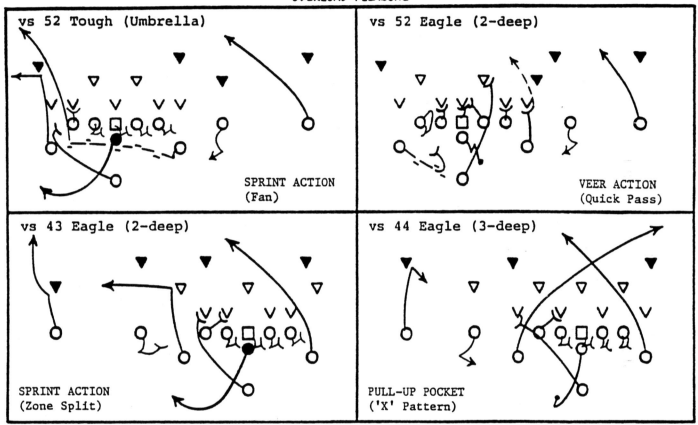

vs 52 Tough (Umbrella)

SPRINT ACTION
(Fan)

vs 52 Eagle (2-deep)

VEER ACTION
(Quick Pass)

vs 43 Eagle (2-deep)

SPRINT ACTION
(Zone Split)

vs 44 Eagle (3-deep)

PULL-UP POCKET
('X' Pattern)

Pass Blocking Schemes and Synopsis of Patterns

Diagram 5 Protection Scheme: Apply Turnback Protection guidelines. The on side tackle first determines the location of the defensive tackle, and then blocks him aggressively with Run blocking techniques.

The on side guard and all other lineman are instructed to pivot to their back side gaps at a 35 degree angle, which positions them to split the outside leg of their innermost lineman and, thereby, to prepare to aggressively engage any defender who crosses in front of their face (zone). Thus, the areas of accountability for the linemen will fall into the following order:

(1) Play side Tackle--block the defensive tackle, (2) Play side Guard--block the A-gap, (3) Center--block the back side A-gap, (4) Back side Short Guard--block the back side B-gap, and (5) Back side Short Tackle--block the back side C-gap.

The fullback is responsible for arc blocking the end man on the line (EMOL). Refer to Chapter III for additional turnback protection insights.

Synopsis: The *Fan* pattern itself is one of the original pass plays from our football heritage.

Slot Back--align at the Strong Side, motion toward the Short Side, and release into the pattern as the first-level receiver from a bending course toward the near goal-line flag/pylon.

Wingback--release into the pattern as the second receiver on a 5-yard bending course into the sideline, which will stretch the flat coverage of the defensive secondary.

Quarterback--roll out to the Short Side flank, determine which receiver is the safest selection of the two, and throw the football quickly. If neither receiver breaks open, throw to the back side split end if in vision, or throw the football safely out of bounds.

- -

Diagram 6 Protection Scheme: Aggressive Hit protection techniques (Chapter III) will apply for the play side slot back, tackle, guard, center and the back side guard and tackle against the down-linemen in their outside-to-inside area of responsibility.

When uncovered, an aforementioned lineman will usually block to the inside and render aid to his inside blocker against a stubborn down lineman. He has the flexibility, however, to block to his outside against an imposing defensive lineman when needed and/or necessary.

The fullback will fake a veer/spike play exchange and then block the on side linebacker.

The ineligible flex end will fake a hitch-pass pivoting movement as a decoy.

The wingback should run an abbreviated twirl motion to protect the back side.

Synopsis: The *Quick Pass* is the most basic of all pass patterns, which exploits the veer/spike action play fake to the fullback.

Quarterback--ride/jab fake with the fullback, take one step to the rear, read the seams that the receivers are slicing, and then quick-fire the football to the open receiver.

Slot Back--although illustrated in a blocking role, he also can release with ease between the inside linebacker and strong safety to run a slant-in route.

Split End--should read the coverage depth of the defensive backs, then run a quick slant-in route between the corner back and strong safety.

- -

Diagram 7 Protection Scheme: Apply Turnback Protection guidelines. The play side tackle first determines the location of the defensive tackle and blocks him aggressively with Run blocking techniques. The play side guard and all other lineman are instructed to pivot to their back side gaps at a 35 degree angle, which positions them to split the outside leg of their innermost lineman and, thereby, to prepare to aggressively engage the defender who crosses in front of their face (zone). Thus, the areas of accountability for the linemen will fall into the following order:

(1) Play side Tackle--block the defensive tackle, (2) Play side Guard-- block the A-gap, (3) Center--block the back side A-gap, (4) Back side Short Guard--block the back side B-gap, and (5) Back side Short Tackle-- block the back side C-gap.

The fullback must arc block the EMOL.

The ineligible flex end will protect his inside area after executing his hitch-pass fake.

Synopsis: The Zone *Split* pattern combines the strong side split end's Up route with his companion slot back's Out route.

The split end's Up (fade) route consists of a 35 degree cut to the outside (inside foot plant), then another cut up the sideline on the third step (outside foot plant).

The slot back's Out route consists of a sharp 45 degree break toward the sideline. When executing the break, his body weight should be brought under control prior to the outside cut, first by widening his steps, and then by planting his inside foot--in conjunction with an inside head feint--before pushing-off forcefully to the outside. A snap of the elbows to the outside helps to sharpen his shift of weight to the outside.

The quarterback should roll-out toward the strong side, and then read the defensive commitment of the corner back. The football's pass trajectory to the split end should have "air" under it, with a slight lead, but a pass made to the slot back during his Out route should have a sharp, low driving trajectory at chest level.

The wingback will run a deep crease route over the middle from the back side, splitting two defensive backs, and should expect a pass thrown to him to occur from the quarterback's own timing process.

- -

Diagram 8 Protection Scheme: Apply Turnback Protection guidelines. The on side tackle first determines the location of the defensive tackle and then blocks him aggressively with Run blocking techniques.

The on side guard and all other lineman are instructed to pivot to their back side gaps at a 35 degree angle, which positions them to split the outside leg of their innermost lineman and, thereby, to prepare them to aggressively engage any defender who crosses in front of their face (zone). Thus, the areas of accountability for the linemen will fall into the following order:

(1) Play side Tackle--block defensive tackle, (2) Play side Guard--block A-gap, (3) Center--block back side A-gap, (4) Back side (Short) Guard-- block the back side B-gap, and (5) Back side (Short) Tackle--block the back side C-gap.

The fullback must kick-out block the EMOL.

Synopsis: The 'X' pattern utilizes the two slot/wing backs on 'X' (crossing) routes, which is effective especially against a man coverage in the secondary.

Slot Back--run a slanting route through the linebacker zone aimed at a depth of 15 yards over the opposite-side wingback area. This course is meant to penetrate through the vulnerable far side coverage crease of the free safety and corner back.

Wingback--run also a slanting course through the linebacker zone, delaying slightly to allow the slot back to cross overhead from the Strong Side, and then sprint into the open zone area located at an approximate depth of 12 yards over the far side tackle.

Split End--run a Hook route into an open void in the zone coverage, usually at an 8-10 yard depth from the back side.

Quarterback--pull-up behind the strong side guard at a 6-yard depth and then read the separation status of the slot back and wingback during their cross over the center area. The ball should be thrown to the selected X-route receiver with a slight lead, so that the intended receiver can "run to the ball" in flight. When the split end is the selected receiver, the pass should be thrown just as he makes his "hook" movement to the inside, with the ball thrown at face mask level (never throw the football above the receiver's forehead, which is the anatomical blind spot area).

PERSONAL MEMORANDA

PERSONAL MEMORANDA

V

A Multiflex Merger

WHY

(A) Multiple sets can be used without creating multiple problems. Varying formations *either* can <u>enhance</u> the blocking strength at the point of attack or <u>divert</u> the defensive coverage away from the attack area. Multiple sets can create a myriad of problems, both for the opposing defenses and their defensive coordinators. These problems include the determination of the the down-and-distance play tendencies that the offense has shown with each alignment and the measures that the defense must take to cope with the varying strengths of each formation.

(B) Power-blocking formations can be blended easily with flexed and spread formations so that their blocking and pass receiving advantages and resulting benefits can be shared without complicating the process. The Multiflex offensive approach is homogeneous, whereas some multiple offensive systems have incompatible mixtures, comparable to the proverbial attempt to mix oil with water.

(C) A select grouping of plays and passes which represent a broad range of "the proven and well-established" can be used with most of the designated alignments. Some plays will perform best, certainly, from a selected choice of alignments than from other less advantageous sets. The Multiflex approach allows the offensive coordinator to "tinker with" a formation disbursement *without changing the play structure of the prescribed offensive format.*

HOW

PRELUDE: There are incalculable ways to identify, name, and disburse formations. The usual method used by coaches involves a system that relies upon descriptive nomenclature. Any terminology that is used to communicate formation deployment is satisfactory *as long as the athletes understand the system and can break from the huddle into the proper formation without becoming confused.* <u>The problem with using descriptive terms to identify formations, however, is that the rhetoric sometimes becomes too wordy when using a variety of formations. This is true particularly when using specialized receivers to deploy the strength of the formation to the split end side at one time and to the tight end side at another time.</u>

THE MULTIFLEX DESIGNATES DIRECTION + HOLE NUMBERS

(A) The signal caller indicates the formation by directing the <u>split end</u> to align either to the "*right*" or to the "*left*" (R/L).

(B) The <u>slot back</u>, who can become a delegated set back or wingback, is directed to align at the location of the called *hole number*.

(C) An added term, such as "tight" (for the flex end) or "flash" (for the set back or fullback), will be included also at appropriate times. Horizontal "fly" motion for the tailback and "motion" and "comeback" motion for the slot back can easily be called upon, as well.

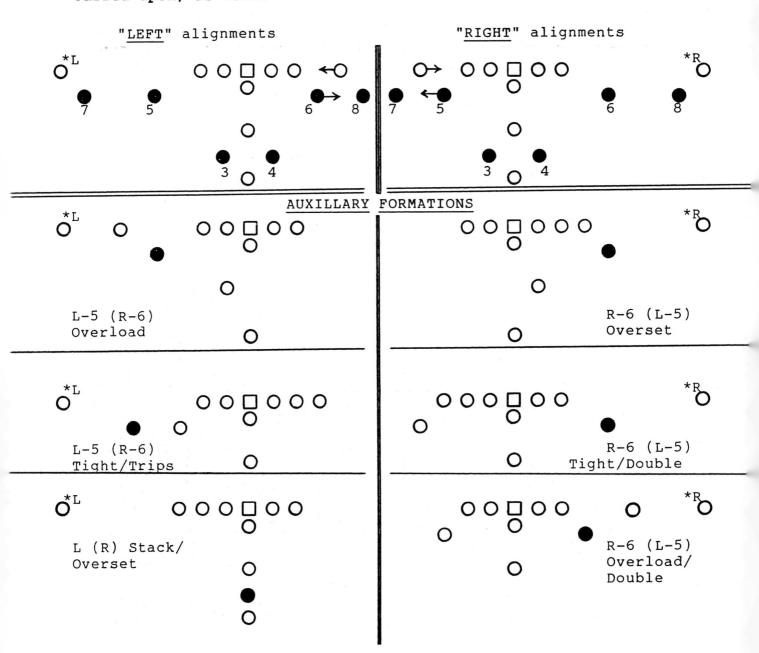

-118-

RATIONALE

The Multiflex approach to the concept of "multiple offense" is the *easiest and least confusing method* that can be used to spread, secure, or "beef-up" the strength of offensive formations WITHOUT destabilizing or changing the basic play format. The Multiflex approach is a very efficient way to eliminate "multiple complications" by insuring that *flexibility of formations is consistently facilitated with an ever-stable, simple method of deployment.*

With the Multiflex approach, team members should NEVER perceive that a formation call is either changing their basic assignments, or changing their basic offense to a less-familiar, different offensive structure. Alignment "calls" may change, but the play structure can remain fundamentally the same WHEN the core system is balanced and soundly structured. Note that the author's recommended play format is capable of striking ALL ATTACK AREAS with variety, yet without needless duplications or interjections of additional assignments or play designs. While there are other methods of designating formation alignments, such as descriptive terms, the Multiflex approach is an adaptable, flexible, and simplified method by which all formation resources and tools can be utilized without getting wordy and/or involved in disrupting offensive structures!

Advantages of Multiflex Concept

(A) The single best advantage of the Multiflex approach to a practical system of multiple offensive, with Slot-I principles preserved included, is that <u>formations can be chosen and emphasized with the physical/talent level of the team's personnel taken into *first* consideration. This can be accomplished without losing sight of the elusive standard of SIMPLICITY!</u> Personnel considerations should include the (1) functional talents of the team's quarterbacks, receivers, and tailback, along with the (2) size and quickness level of the fullback and offensive linemen.

(B) The basic play format, communication system, and weekly game plans do not need to undergo radical changes, considering that the slot back's varying alignments is the factor that will determine the changes in the formation's structural alignment. *Since the <u>slot back</u> sometimes will be <u>removed from the linemen's blocking-scheme structure</u>, there will be a need to make a line call to <u>change</u> the blocking scheme. The blocking scheme to use should be decided by the offensive coordinator. If a change in blocking scheme becomes necessary once the lineman break from the huddle and line up on the line of scrimmage, it should be verbalized by a designated lineman, such as the center or play side guard!* The blocking scheme choices are covered in the play-assignment section portraying and illustrating the Flexing

Offense (Chapter I). The blocking schemes adapted for the comprehensive Multiflex attack are specified in the chart entitled 'Composite of Play Assignments,' which is located on page 130 of this chapter.

(C) Line-call alternatives are neither difficult to teach nor implement, providing they are (1) Included in the early training stages of a new season, and (2) Taught with patience through demonstrations, illustrative diagrams, and "walk through" rehearsals on the practice field. A *learning reinforcement* should be covered on a WEEKLY BASIS for all blocking situations. This teaching process is important, especially, for (1) The slow-to-learn, (2) Those who do not retain information for a lengthy time, and, in general, (3) The team as a group to insure their "athletic sharpness" through frequent field reviews of the participant's playing cues and techniques.

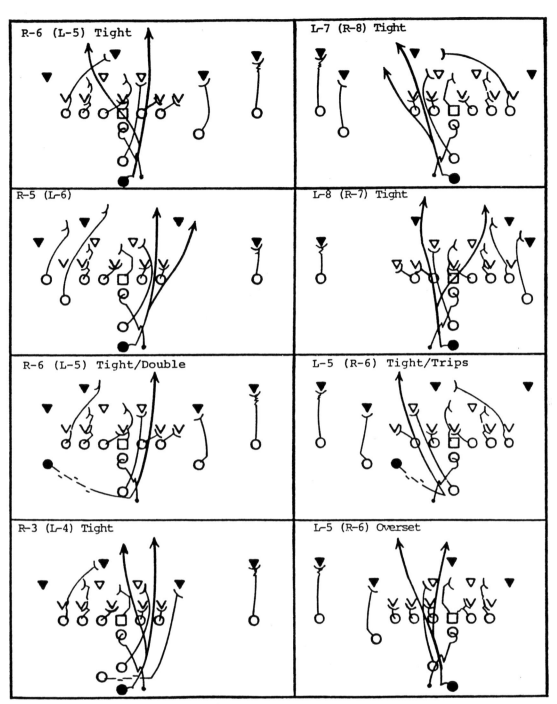

WHAM (Linebacker Isolation)

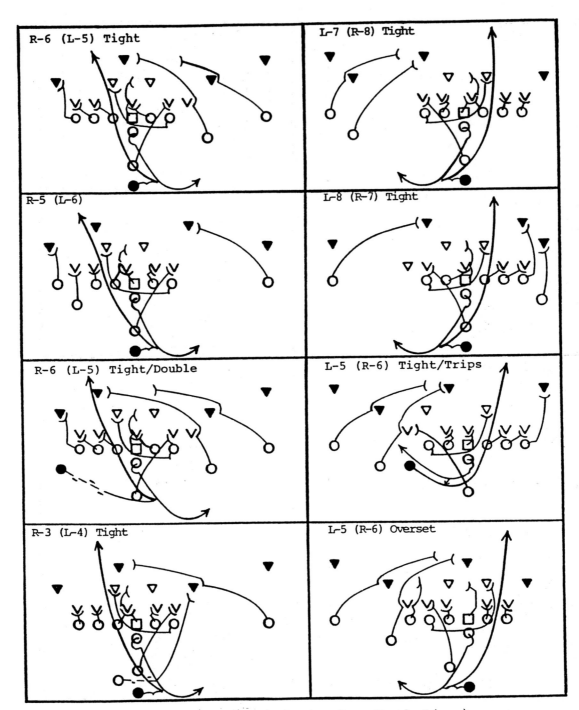

COUNTER WHAM (Linebacker Isolation)

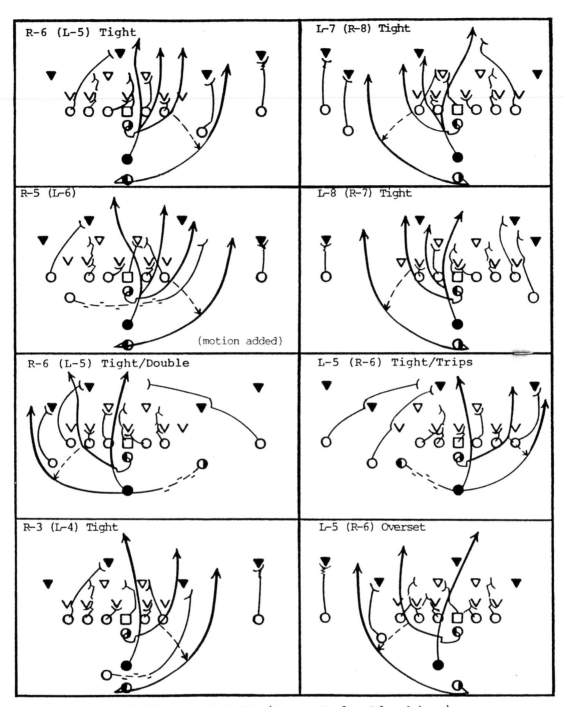

SPIKE + OPTION (Area-Rule Blocking)

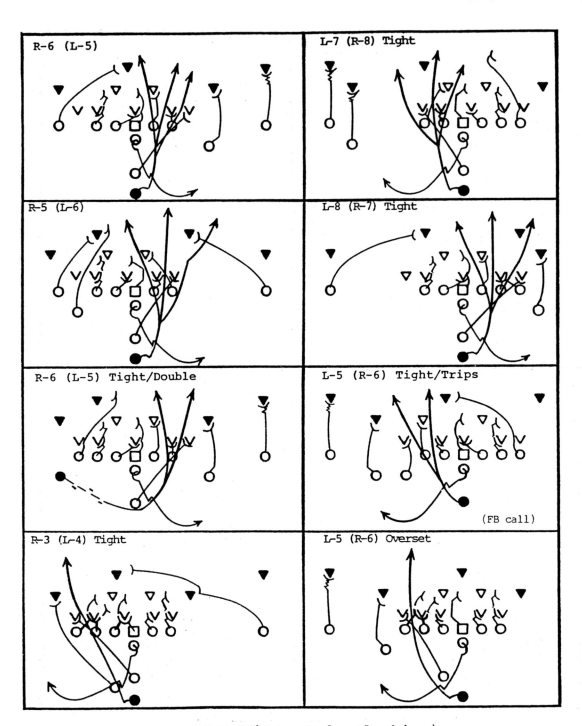

SLANT (Area Rule Blocking)

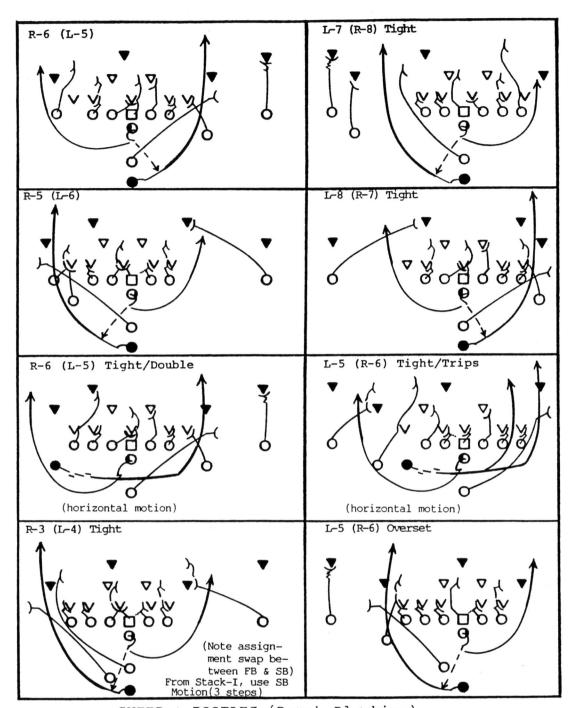

R-6 (L-5)

L-7 (R-8) Tight

R-5 (L-6)

L-8 (R-7) Tight

R-6 (L-5) Tight/Double

L-5 (R-6) Tight/Trips

(horizontal motion)

(horizontal motion)

R-3 (L-4) Tight

L-5 (R-6) Overset

(Note assign-
ment swap be-
tween FB & SB)
From Stack-I, use SB
Motion(3 steps)

SWEEP + BOOTLEG (Reach Blocking)

ADAPTING ZONE BLOCKING PRINCIPLES TO AREA RULE AND REACH BLOCKING SITUATIONS for the Slant, Spike Option, and Sweep/Bootleg plays

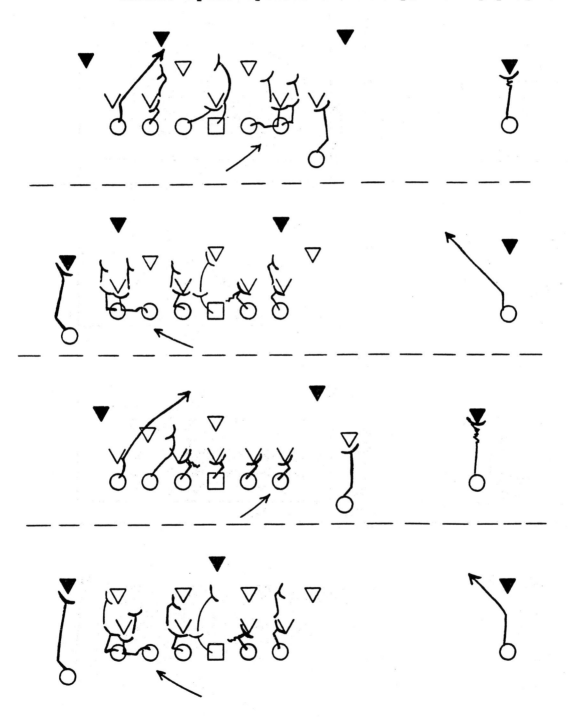

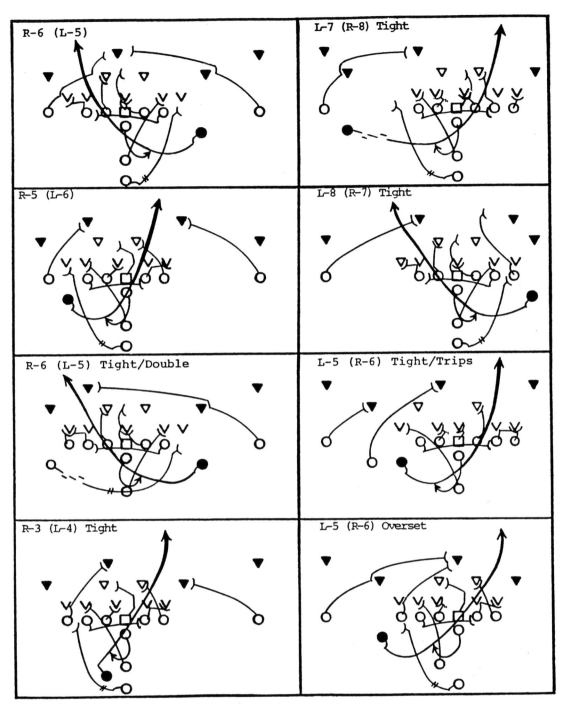

R-6 (L-5)

L-7 (R-8) Tight

R-5 (L-6)

L-8 (R-7) Tight

R-6 (L-5) Tight/Double

L-5 (R-6) Tight/Trips

R-3 (L-4) Tight

L-5 (R-6) Overset

TACKLE TRAP

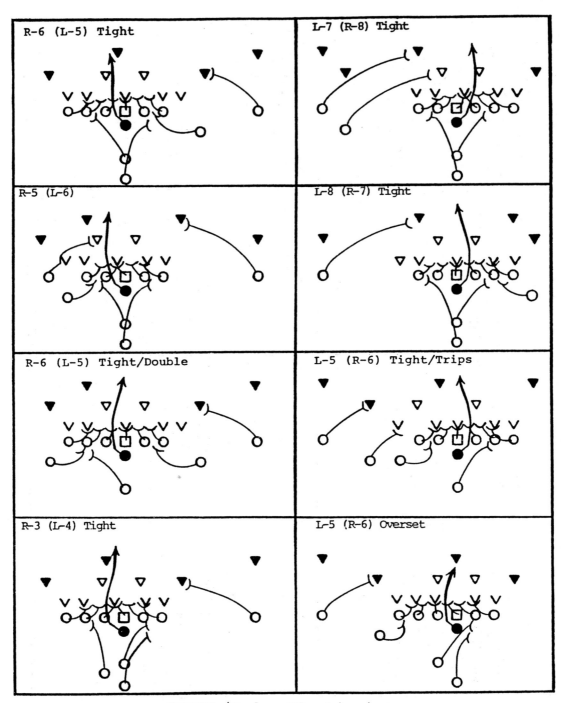

GOOSE (Wedge Blocking)

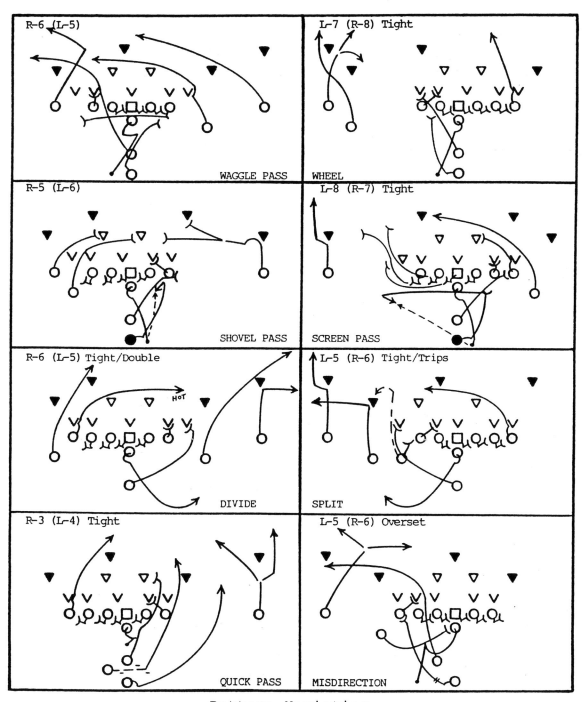

-Pattern Varieties-

COMPOSITE OF PLAY ASSIGNMENTS

PLAY	CENTER	PSG	PST	PSSB/PSTE	PSSE	BSG	BST	FB
WHAM (Lead Draw w/ILB Isolate)	Block Play Side Track: Cut off gap/LB. If no NG/DL, or if NG slides to play side, go to 2nd level.	Block the #1 defender on line-of-scrimmage (disregard linebacker).	Block the #2 defender on line-of-scrimmage (disregard linebacker).	SB blocks the Covering OLB or SS; The TE blocks the CB or OLB. Gap calls: SB & TE block DE.	Block CB vs 3-deep; NS vs 4-deep.	Block Down Line-man Zone: A-gap, Over, Back Side	Rake and Re-lease: Rake B-gap to 2nd level	Lead Block play side ILB.
COUNTER WHAM (Counter Draw/w ILB Isolate)	(guidelines above)	(guidelines above)	(guidelines above)	(guidelines above)	(guidelines above)	(guidelines above)	Pull play side and Lead Block on side ILB.	Fill the back side B-gap.
SPIKE + SPIKE OPTION (Area Rule)	(guidelines above)	Block #1 defender.	Block #2 defender.	SB: Block OLB/SS. TE: Block OLB or CB.	Force Block the CB	(guidelines above)	Rake & Re-lease guide-lines.	Run-ner/play fake
SLANT (Area Rule/w TE Power)	(guidelines above)	(guidelines above).	(guidelines above).	TE: "Down Block" in-side. SB: Block the SS/OLB.	Block CB vs 3-deep; NS vs 4-deep.	(guidelines above)	(guidelines above)	Kick-Out Block on side DE.
SWEEP + BOOTLEG (Reach Block)	(guidelines above).	(guidelines above or line-call to G-Pull)	Reach Block covering defender.	Reach Block DE/OLB when split.	(guidelines above)	(guidelines above)	(guidelines above)	Block Corner Support (CB, SS, or OLB)
TACKLE TRAP (Middle Trap)	(guidelines above).	Block #1 defender; if trap target, Exit Block to outside.	Block the inside/middle linebacker. If LB is #1, Exit Block to outside.	TE: Block the DE. If flexed, Crack Block to inside.	(guidelines above)	(guidelines above)	Pull and Trap Block past cen-ter.	Fill Block back side B-gap.
GOOSE (Wedge Block)	ALL LINEMEN: Either the Center or Play Side Guard, whichever is covered, will SURGE forward as the APEX blocker in the wedge. All remaining linemen—and the Slot Back—will PINCH INSIDE on the snap of the football (silent count), in-terlock inside shoulder pad with outside shoulder pad of blocker in front and become a part of a massive, moving wedge of blockers! The idea is to get momen-tum, and thereby force the defenders to lose traction and retreat backwards. The slot back must decide whether to arc inside the C-gap or Down-Block inside upon the defensive end. The FB and TB secure their on side/back side C-gaps.							
Turnback Protec-tion...	Hinge Block back side (BS) A-gap.	Hinge Block back side (BS) A-gap.	Block DT w/ aggressive 'Hit' tech.	Assigned pass route.	Assig-ned route.	Hinge BS A-gap.	Hinge BS C-gap.	Climb Block DE.

-130-

SUBSTITUTING THE LOAD-BLOCK VEER FOR THE SPIKE OPTION

A SECURE TRIPLE-OPTION ADDITION

With the inclusion of the Load-block Veer play in the place of the two-way Spike Option, a core format of seven reliable plays can be emphasized as the foundation of the Multiflex offensive attack. This solid-seven format of plays can be drilled to a level of near perfection in the execution of technique. This format can be supported further with a supplemental set of three additional plays to assure dependability in sustaining lengthily drives. The original composition of the Multiflex formula remains unchanged, however, which includes draw, misdirection, option, power-principle, and the straight-thrust plays that jointly attack all areas along the defensive front.

The plays listed below are from the basic structure of the *Flexing Offense* which illustrate the "seven plus three" rationale when the manipulative Load Veer play is a part of this elite Multiflex agenda.

1) WHAM (tailback lead draw)

2) COUNTER WHAM (tailback counter draw)

3) SLANT (tailback strike inside defensive end)

4) SPIKE (fullback quick-opener with tailback counter-movement)

5) LOAD VEER (an optional fullback dive, or quarterback keeper, or tailback pitch runner along the on side flank)

6) TACKLE TRAP (slot back scissor)

7) SWEEP (tailback downhill toss)

    +BOOTLEG (quarterback keeper opposite fake of sweep)

    +GOOSE (quarterback drive behind interior wedge blockers)

    +COUNTER REVERSE (slot back wide reverse)

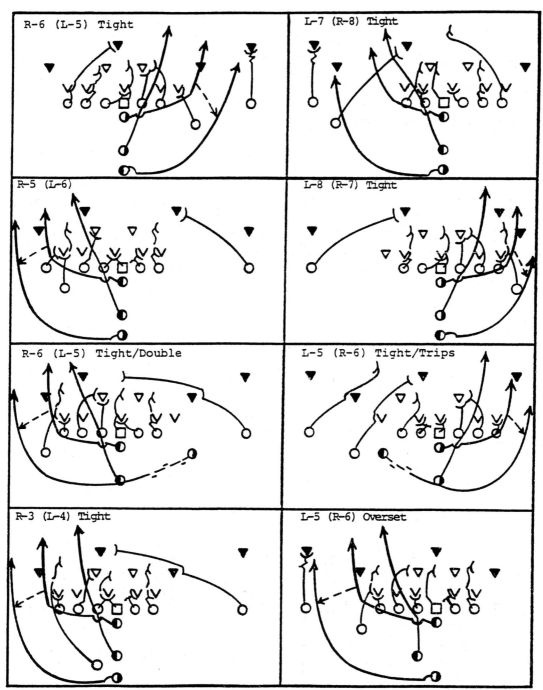

R-6 (L-5) Tight

L-7 (R-8) Tight

R-5 (L-6)

L-8 (R-7) Tight

R-6 (L-5) Tight/Double

L-5 (R-6) Tight/Trips

R-3 (L-4) Tight

L-5 (R-6) Overset

LOAD VEER

LOAD VEER (a "secure" three-way triple option)

Blocking Scheme: PSSE--force block corner support; PSTE/SB--load block the pitch key (first opponent outside the read key). When the slot back is aligned as a set back or wingback, he first will secure the block of his tight end upon the pitch key and then advance to the nearest deep safety; PST--block the inside linebacker; PSG--block the #1 defender; Center--block the play side track; BSG--block the down lineman zone; BST--rake & release to 2nd level.

Guiding Technique: The quarterback can use a "fail safe" exchange technique (step with on side foot, point the football behind the buttocks of the on side guard, then withdraw the football just PRIOR to the arrival of the fullback IF the defensive read-key's shoulders are pointing inside, which signals his pre-snap commitment to defend the inside. Otherwise, HAND THE BALL OFF TO THE FULLBACK!). The Load Veer is meant to be a powerful fullback plunge, first, and an optional play, second. Since the pitch key is subdued with a load block, the option read is extended a play hole wider, with the outside key to become the first secondary defender to challenge the quarterback. The tailback must maintain a constant pitch relationship with his quarterback at a depth and lateral width of four yards and should expect the option-pitch to take place within a level in the defensive secondary. *The Load Veer can be executed by a quarterback with average reflexes and moderate running adeptness because the applied load block from his on side tight end or slot back will virtually nullify the threat of a "crashing" defensive end.*

FORMATIONAL STRATEGIES

(A) Consider the basic Slot-I alignment, with a tight end and flexed slot back, as a dependable and reliable formation that can be called upon in most any situation, from the defensive to the offensive goal line. This implied security is in reference to both passing and running plays, alike.

(1) Usage of a flexed tight end should best be utilized in the open field and when approaching the offensive goal line. Be reluctant, therefore, to flex a tight end when backed up against the opponent's goal line, or in any situation that is invitational to blitzing linebackers or gap penetration by the defensive linemen.

(2) When deciding to flex the tight end in any precarious situation, take into account the defensive adjustments that should be anticipated, the passing efficiency of the quarterback, and how seriously the opposing secondary honors the receivers.

(B) Consider the closed-formation sets, with the running backs and/or receivers in tight, as the better alignments to depend upon when located near *either* goal line. This is true, especially, when "backed-up" within the area of the opponent's goal line (Red Zone) in which a miscue and/or loss of possession (turnover) could have disastrous results. Closed formations are valuable in the final minutes of a football game when ahead in score and the emphasis needs to be placed upon (1) protecting the football from a turnover and (2) running-out the remaining time on the clock.

(C) Consider the spread-formation sets, with a liberal usage of wide-receiver arrangements, as the better alignments to depend upon when located in the open-field Green Zone. Wide alignments tend to be more effective on first and second down within the scoring area near the offensive goal line (Blue Zone). Power-I and Overset alignments also are worthy of consideration in the Blue Zone (described below). Spread-formation sets should have preference over closed-formation sets late in the game and behind in the score. A talented, but physically bruised, running back also can be deployed as a wide receiver if he possesses reliable pass-catching hands.

(D) In regard to formation decisions within the Blue Zone, if the offensive team is made up of physically-small athletes, primarily, carefully evaluate the use of tight alignments when attempting to run inside. If the opposition defense has an advantage in physical size, a tight offensive formation may only *solidify* the defensive "brick wall" by tightening the defenders.

FOUR FIELD-POSITION ZONES DESIGNATED FOR RUN/PASS ATTACKS

(A) RED (DANGER) ZONE: Designated from the opponent's goal line (defensive) to the -15 yard line (85 yards to score). Think in terms of getting the football safely out of this critical area. Avoid the use of pulling linemen whenever possible, since this invites defensive penetration. Recommend usage of a tight-end Slot-I, or any Multiflex variation that maximizes blocking security, such as a Power-I alignment. Play calls should NOT involve anything that is intricate! The passing game should generally favor Roll Outs and Play Action, such as the Quick Pass. Pull Up Passes tend to be risky because the opposing defense may be tempted to use pressuring tactics such as gap crashes, linemen loops, and linebacker blitzes. A good antidote to such defensive tactics, however, is make use of the Shovel and perhaps a Screen Pass (strictly judgment calls).

(B) YELLOW (CAUTION) ZONE: Designated from the -15 yard line to the -35 yard line (65 yards to score). Since there is "breathing room" from the opponent's goal line (at least fifteen yards to the rear), think in terms of moving the football forward to the Green Zone (beginning at the +35 yard line) with generally conservative formations and play calls that are not "high-risk." A fumble or interception "turnover" that changes the ball possession to the opposition can be costly, so it is wise not to spread the blocking forces too thin. It is usually prudent to use formations that keep the ends secured in this area and to stay away from "desperation" quick-scoring attempts, unless behind in the score and the remaining game time is about to run out.

(C) GREEN (FREE-SCORING) ZONE: Designated from the -35 yard line to the +35 yard line. Think in terms of utilizing spread receivers. Open up all running play and passing game resources! Pull Up Passes should now become an integral part of the repertoire of attack weapons, along with Play Action and Roll Out Action Passes. Now is the time to mix up plays, attempting to make the calls that the opposition is not expecting, and to run and pass where the opposition is vulnerable. Be careful to stay within the boundaries of reliable, sound judgment, however, because earned first downs and timely touchdowns IS the primary objective!

(D) BLUE (4-DOWN) ZONE: Designated from the +35 yard line to the offensive goal line. Since the offense has an extra down to utilize, usually without the necessity to strategically punt on fourth down, the "free-scoring" plays that are planned for the Green Zone (above) can be given their full opportunity to score.

(1) Exceptions to this thinking should apply when faced with critical short-yardage play situations, and when the opposing defense is backed up against its defending goal line, whereas the defending territory in the secondary is compressed. Short-yardage and goal-line play selections should be conservative, a majority

of the time, to the extent that the plays strike with directness and/or with power-blocking principles. On the goal line, plays such as the Wedge (quarterback sneak) and the tailback Wham (isolation) are time proven selections to consider.

(2) Sometimes sweeps and wide reverse plays are a good choice, but the defensive tendencies first should be examined and evaluated very carefully. Play-action Quick Passes and Roll Out Pass patterns directed into the flats (horizontal zone stretch principle) generally are fail-safe, reliable pass play calls.

AXIOMS FOR RUN/PASS OFFENSIVE FOOTBALL

(A) Go for big gains within the Green and Blue Zones on first and second down! Third down should be reserved for the most dependable plays that can be called upon to make the needed first down.

(B) Intimidate, and thereby loosen, the defensive coverage of the opposition with a balanced offensive threat of running and passing!

(C) Attempt to get the opposing defensive unit into your play-sequence rhythm! When the defense gets caught up into an offensive rhythm, game control is on the side of the play caller.

(D) Place maximum pressure on the opposing defense immediately after the opponent loses ball possession from a sudden turnover!

(E) Guard against setting play-calling trends with pet plays! Use change-of-pace plays to keep the opposing defense unsure about what to expect next. Interweave quick openers, power, and misdirection plays with the passing attack! (Please refer to "Strategy" in Chapter II for specific usage of plays)

(F) Remember that special plays should remain just that-- special! An over use of special plays will tend to nullify their effectiveness and, as a result, an untimely turnover could occur.

(G) Control and exploit the opponent's secondary coverage with a usage of slot back Motion and Comeback Motion, tailback Fly motion, and fullback Flash motion to "pre-stretch" the defense horizontally before releasing the receivers into the secondary either on a pass pattern or on an isolated, individual route. In this way, receiver leverages can be evaluated and thus explored against each pass coverage, along with their adjustments.

(H) Keep in mind that the best way to run on a defensive unit is to loosen it first with a pass! This is true especially when running an option offense. The best way to pass on a defensive unit is to tighten it first with a run! A clever play caller will usually sense when it is necessary to "bunch up" the offensive formations and when to "spread out." Confidence, intuition, and initiative can carry an average team to above average heights. The signal caller must have a *mental image* of what he is attempting to accomplish, and have the *resolve* of a clearly defined philosophy of the navigational offense that he intends to direct and manage.

(I) Prepare to adjust to changing circumstances that will inevitably take place during highly competitive games! In spite of big-play aspirations, there will be circumstances when the offense must control the time on the clock and maintain possession of the football with low risk, high percentage plays, especially when struggling in poor field position at the closing moments of a ball game. Other factors to consider when deciding to use clock (ball) control measures include the (1) personnel equation whereas the opponent clearly has the advantage in manpower and/or talent, and, also (2) when injuries to key personnel has affected the firepower potential of the offense or the stability of the defensive unit. When undertaking clock control measures, it is important to focus upon <u>consistency</u> in order to keep the offensive drive alive without making careless mistakes. *Successful clock control during a game can usually be attributed to disciplined training in practice sessions with the emphasis on cool-headed concentration and attention to detail.*

PERSONAL MEMORANDA

PERSONAL MEMORANDA

VI

MANAGEMENT and AFTERTHOUGHTS

Value of Pragmatic Drills

Football drills are an essential function in the development of the game's necessary skills. Each and every drill, therefore, should have at least one specific purpose. The most efficient drills, however, will accomplish several major objectives and a few minor ones, as well, such as agility and reaction, conditioning, morale building, etc.

Specialty workout periods, especially, should be designed to incorporate as many multi-purpose skill-development objectives that are practical. The vital skills of the center-snap, kicking, kick-off receiving, punting, punt receiving, and the return skills of the above, in example, should be combined. The important technique skills for the offensive linemen also can be combined, such as one-on-one blocking in conjunction with follow-up applications of first-to-second level blocking assignments. For the defensive linemen, the vast array of rip, anchor, pursue, slant and "lock-up" form-tackling techniques can be combined easily and effectively in drill sessions.

Unit time can then be spent on defensive pass interceptions, used in combination with follow-up blocking procedures. Then, at a separate time, time can be spent on offensive reaction, defensive recovery and tackling situations and procedures whenever a "sudden turnover" from a pass interception occurs.

If a drill does not relate specifically to a scrimmage or game maneuver, then time should NOT be spent on it. During a coaching staff meeting, take the necessary time to evaluate the structural make up, safety control, function and the player interaction of each and every drill *before* making an attempt to use it on the practice field.

The design of practice drills for any sport should be PRAGMATIC! This means that a drill should take a practical approach to achieving a goal, to accomplish an objective, to solve a technique or physical reaction problem, or to improve the mental recognition of the alignments and tactics of the opponent. With the above kept in perspective, field coaches should be vigilant in overseeing and safeguarding the field conditions that are involved in all drill-time applications.

Spring and Summer Workouts

One of the most productive and time-saving decisions that a head coach can make is to plot the direction and substance of the spring and pre-season summer practice sessions. Input from all the assistant coaches is desirable due to the added insight that can be gained, plus other probable benefits such as an improvement in the thrifty usage of time spent on the field, and an encouragement to staff members to make meaningful contributions-- which, in turn, can promote staff togetherness and loyalty.

There are a multitude of approaches and philosophies in processing a practice schedule design, but an important practical step to consider first should be to structure a near-permanent outline of <u>time-periods</u> that will be reserved religiously for specific drill areas and facets of the overall game. If a time allotment is specified and set aside on a generic, daily practice chart, important and vital areas such as the kicking game, option drill skills, etc., should never be inadvertently overlooked. The prime objective, in essence, should be to set aside designated time periods to cover all the vital segments of the game, such as (1) "Position Skills," (2) "Unit Work," and (3) "Team Time," which must include time allotments for both offense and defense. With the time periods CHARTED, the specified drills that are to be emphasized on a given day can then be filled-in with a pencil on generalized time-allotment forms or charts.

Some coaches prefer to schedule certain days of the week solely to cover the kicking game or offense or defense, exclusively. This plan has its merits, and it certainly can be implemented on occasion to break a monotony of routine. There is a risk, however, in using a "day of the week" plan entirely in the pre-season due to the need to develop <u>all</u> fundamental areas of the game in <u>short sessions</u> of learning and to review situations on a day-by-day basis, for maximum retention. To insure that the athletes maintain their crispness, it is important that all pertinent fundamental areas of the game are "touched upon" on a regular basis.

It is important, also, to protect the team against possible problems of absenteeism that may occur, such as an illness of key players--or even, unauthorized absenses--in which the "main duty" workouts are missed. This specific problem can have a definite effect on the overall productivity of the entire team. But, whatever plan of work schedule finally is adopted, remember that the "whole game" can reach a state of precision only by developing the quality of its "parts" on a consistent, regular basis.

Seasonal Workouts

Most high school coaches, as a general rule, seem to prefer the "day-of-the-week" practice routine or structure for their in-season workouts. With the game of the week scheduled for Friday, in example, the following guidelines would be applicable and worthy of consideration...

1) Monday could be spent in "half pads" with the emphasis and tutoring focused upon the information gathered in the scout report, to explain the tendencies of the opposition and the necessary adjustments that must be made. Time also could be spent in the areas of passing and receiving, pass coverage, option-play finesse, and all components of the kicking game.

2) Tuesday could be spend in full pads, with a heavy emphasis placed on a three-level approach--specialty, unit and team--serving both the offensive and defensive needs in preparing for the upcoming game.

3) Wednesday could be spent again in full pads, however, with lighter contact. This can be a good day to "fine tune" all facets of the offense and defense, alike, and also to cover selected parts of the kicking game, such as live punting and punt returns, etc.

Note: Some coaches have shown a preference to spending their in-season Tuesdays on defense and reserve Wednesdays for offense, exclusively.

4) Thursday could be spent solely on kicking-game coverages, pre-game warm up orientation and/or recaps that dwell on play TIMING. A review of the "check lists" for the special teams and their backup replacements also should be covered at this time.

Note: Thursday and Monday evenings both are ideal for scheduling junior varsity contests. For those who play scheduled contests on Saturdays, Mondays could be spent wisely on film reviews, scout report critiques both on and off the practice field, and on fun-oriented conditioning drills such as relays, pass receiving contests between offensive and defensive groups, and/or "warrior games" between the linemen and the skill positions, such as tug-of-war, etc. Then the daily schedules mentioned above could be moved-up by one day (in example, the Thursday schedule will be moved-up to Friday).

Pre-Game Routine

Football teams at present seem to have a structured pre-game warm up routine with specialized time segments that emphasize small-group situational reviews, along with the relevant, light-duty maneuvers, reactions, and drill repetitions that can be used to ready their athletes for the awaiting game. The first to enter the field, usually, are the kicking game specialists, which includes all the kick off, punting, and extra point/field goal kickers, plus their "support personnel" such as the deep snappers, holders, and the kick off and punt return runners. The quarterbacks, receivers, defensive backs, and linebackers will usually become a part of this designated "early specialists" group. This time period usually is informal and personalized, but supervised.

When the remainder of the team merges with the early specialists, "unit work" usually begins under the supervision and guidance of the position coaches. This segment usually involves recognition, reaction, agility and assignment drills that apply specifically to the game, in a break-down version, for the members of each unit. This unit work is designed to relate to all linemen and backs, both offensively and defensively.

At the conclusion of the unit warm up period, a brief "team time" period for the offense and defense, alike, will often follow, with an emphasis placed upon "polish work" timing and an overall team review. When this wrap-up time concludes, the team then will usually report to the sideline.

All time allotments should be brief and both highly organized and disciplined. The overall organization positively must include the duties of the team managers and trainers, plus their accessibility to all the necessary equipment hardware, medical supplies, and professional medical services.

Stability of Program

One of the very difficult problems that face junior/senior high school coaches, presently, is that of holding a "team family" together when the athletes are out-of-season for one sport, but are playing in-season for another coach and sport. Football coaches often can rely upon the other sports to continue a developmental program to improve the status of player strength and general agility and jumping skills, to some extent, but the problem of keeping "close ties" still remains and it does need to be addressed without infringing upon another team's rights, jurisdiction and focus. Realistic progress in the development of football players will take place, however, ONLY when the football coaching staff takes an active and involved role in out-of-season developmental workouts for their athletes. These workouts should be scheduled during appropriate "free time" and positively should NEVER be endeavored at the expense of another coach or his/her sport! To be successful, out-of-season workouts should have a short time span and, also, be an activity of fun and internally competitive for the participants.

A school's administration, as a critical starting point, should give it's blessings and support to all "year round" development programs for their entire sports agenda. To assure fairness and eliminate conflict, the programs MUST BE CONTROLLED and SUPERVISED by someone in a position of authority! The coaches who are directly involved should be the ones to meet as a group, agree upon a coordinating process and cooperate with each other. Coaches should be sensitive to the fact that most of the premier athletes often will be in transition from one sport to another as the seasons change, and SOMEWHERE along the way they need a mental and physical "break" in order to function at their best and enjoy their participation and contribution. It is a MORAL responsibility of all coaches in the profession to be fair and just to their athletes by encouraging an involvement in other activities, and to work together in the coordination of the student athlete's out-of-season workouts.

If administrative backing fails to be brought into the process, however, there will be great difficulty in running a truly successful year-round program that realistically will benefit all athletes. Administrative backing is more readily secured, however, if the implied purpose of the conditioning program is to prevent injury, as well as enhance performance. In most leagues, the competition among rival schools across this country is usually keen, therefore it is near mandatory to have a quality out-of-season workout program in order to win with consistency from year-to-year.

We should remember, collectively, that athletic programs are sanctioned for the BETTERMENT and FULFILLMENT of the student athletes as they strive to fulfill their educational, social, psychological, and spiritual desires and goals. Our American school systems and their adjacent community recreational departments should take a joint responsibility in providing wholesome and meaningful activities to occupy the free time of our young people and, thereby, eliminate the negative distractions and pitfalls that presently face adolescents today. All community school boards and administrations hold the power to approve and enact all athletic activities, but it is the coaches that hold the key to the responsiveness and enthusiasm of the student athletes.

Winners and Losers

It is an innate part of our human instinct to seek the challenge and thrill of competition! There is an inner craving within most of us to experience the satisfaction and the gratification of achievement and its resulting success in our ventures and relationships. To ride the crest of a tidal wave of glory, to capture the adoration and affection of others, and especially to build a successful family unit and prosperous occupational enterprise with an influential and lasting legacy is something that most Americans seek and pursue. To experience victory and/or success is to hold an essential building-block that contributes to the development of self-esteem. To feel accepted and appreciated also in an important catalyst that can bring out an inner sense of "feeling good about ourselves."

There also is a human tendency to embrace sports for an opportunity to experience positive feelings of accomplishment, victory and a development of character traits. Players and coaches, alike, seek to gain these feelings of zeal through their game experiences, while spectators and fans tend to gain their personal feelings of worthiness through their identification to a team group, and through their booster support.

Our ego and sense of pride compels us to overcome obstacles ahead and to experience the realization of a distinguishable TRIUMPH OVER DEFEAT! To the "doers" who contribute the most to a victorious achievement, the <u>ultimate satisfaction</u> lies within these individuals, since their reward includes the self-satisfaction in knowing that their dedication, unwavering determination and work ethics have reaped *the full harvest* of victory. Added dividends of appreciative, heart-warming accolades also may follow from the alumni, fans, and student body.

As for the "flip-side of the coin," a coach or entrepreneur certainly could invest as much research, management, intense effort, and personal involvement into his/her coaching or business ventures as realistically possible, and yet fall short in the "success column." A successful and productive year may well be followed by a less successful one, though the work energies may be nearly the same--in fact, most of us work harder when our business life is not doing well ("When the going gets tough, the tough get going").

Variables will always exist that will determine the present status of one's success or failure. The end-result of any circumstance or test of competition will be determined, usually, by such components as the caliber of competition, the available resources, the time factor, and, certainly, the sheer element of luck--which often occurs when "preparation meets with opportunity." To the winner goes the covetous "spoils of victory," while the loser fails neither to receive or enjoy the anticipated rewards that were sought after in his/her quest for victory and continued success.

Most coaches/career people will experience the "hills and valleys of success and failure," while a majority of us probably will linger somewhere between the two, traveling on a roadway over "rolling hills." For most of us, neither the "peaks" nor the "trenches" are a firm reality. We do have the free will and intellect, as humans, to overcome both the circumstances and the conditions of hardships by seeking-out the knowledge that is needed and necessary, and then apply the spirit and drive that will facilitate the upswing to achievement. Life itself is a challenge, and this is what makes us GROW as individual personalities. We must, therefore, have the capabilities and necessities to ADJUST and ENDURE because the real or imaginary plane that separates the "high and low" experiences of life is usually vacillating, therefore a renewed opportunity to succeed is usually within our grasp. As the great Chinese philosopher Confucius once said over two thousand years ago, *"Our greatest glory consists not in never falling, but in rising every time we fall."*

Mission and Purpose

There is a timeless expression among high school coaches that we, as "professional educators," are verbally hired for one reason (such as "teaching and development of character") and then fired later for the true "bottom line" reason (not winning enough games and/or not remaining "politically correct" with the power elite). With this in mind, perhaps there are two "worlds" in which coaches live--the noble and the real!

When a coach makes his debut into a new coaching-job venture, a "honeymoon" of sorts usually prevails for a while until the season gets under way. During this "honeymoon" state of well-being, a newly-hired head coach can begin to implant a standard of excellence with implied values that will set the tempo for character and athletic development. This is the time, generally, when team enthusiasm and hopes are renewed, and many team policies and management techniques also can be reworked. The athletic complex and its facilities, as well, are often refurbished at this time.

If early-season "confidence" wins are fortunate to take place, the momentum gained can help to keep the program on a positive, successful track. When the euphoria begins to wane, however, problem areas that once could have been whisked aside now suddenly must be dealt with. This is because the present "level of happiness" will seem to lose its splendor and any verbalized justification given for past "discomforts and inconveniences" now will tend to fall upon "deaf ears," while the mentality of "what have you done for me lately" will rule the day.

If a season begins to experience a slump, petty jealousies, internal school politics, and certain *innuendoes* for favoritism, for some "unknown reason," may begin to surface "all of a sudden." The hardest task of all, sometimes, is to convince both the student athletes and their parents that there should be both a (1) Personal investment and a commitment made in behalf of the athlete for the purpose of developing himself and, also, to make a (2) Contribution of effort and leadership to the team. This is important, especially, when the team's present "inventory" of available team talent is not as rich in resources as can be found in rival organizations, or if the athletes are comparatively young and/or inexperienced.

In spite of this, the rationale to win sometimes is aggressively pushed to its limits, and often at the expense of traditional values. Negative pressures often are imposed upon coaches, both from the fans and school personnel. These situations become the hard times of the "real world" that a coach sometimes must deal with, but the mentally tough will only bend like a pine tree in the wind, and will seldom break. An embattled coach, in fact, will usually "snap back" into an upright posture when the storm recedes, just as in the case of the tall tree. Because the football coaches of this country basically ARE a breed that's mentally tough, they have the necessities to withstand the worst of times, within reason, yet too many coaches in the profession seem to allow unwarranted abuses from self-righteous people. No individual or group has the right to inflict either insult or any form of subtle assault upon a coach, a coach's family, the team members, or against any school personnel, for that matter.

Having put the "bottom line" pressures of winning aside, there still remains a cardinal principle: OUR MISSION AND PURPOSE AS COACHES OF ADOLESCENT ATHLETES IS TO DEVELOP EACH AND EVERY YOUNGSTER TO THE ZENITH OF HIS/HER POTENTIAL AND PERSONAL SELF-ESTEEM! WHILE TRYING TO REALIZE THIS MISSION, ALWAYS ATTEMPT TO BE AS FAIR AS HUMANLY POSSIBLE, FIRST TO THE TEAM AS A WHOLE AND, SECONDLY, TO EACH PLAYER COLLECTIVELY AS A MEMBER OF THE TEAM AND AS AN INDIVIDUAL!

Through a fortification of each player's self-esteem and of the team (family) as a whole, PRIDE can be developed and <u>then</u> player character can be built! When pride is established, positive "links of the chain" can be added in the form of confident attitudes, a faith in one's self, and a faith in the team's ability to perform under pressure. When a self-assured certainty has been developed in the combat competence and reaction skills of the team members, a cohesive spirit within the team is a near certainty--and one of the vital links to success is in place. Confident athletic attitudes, however, are <u>acquired</u> only through REGIMEN, RITUAL, GUIDANCE, and <u>POSITIVE REINFORCEMENT</u>!

PERSONAL MEMORANDA

PERSONAL MEMORANDA

BIBLIOGRAPHY

The primary purpose of this bibliographical account is to give credit to the many coaches who have made invaluable contributions to offensive football, especially to the development of I-formation attacks. Secondary purposes includes an attempt to validate and authenticate the author by a disclosure of his four-decade background of <a> Experience in coaching, <b> Collection and procurement of literary material, <c> Abreast monitoring of the ongoing developments in the game of football, and <d> continuing research and background of exposure to a vast array of the football coaching clinics, films, and videotapes that have enlightened the profession.

Football coaches are commonly known to share and interchange information through mutual conversation, seminars, written presentations, exchange of game films and videotapes, exchange of methods and techniques, and insights into defeating a scheduled opponent. Not only have coaching clinics played a big part in the author's professional education, televised football games--and their highlights--have provided a wealth of football knowledge.

With this having been said, it is near impossible, sometimes, to clarify the true origin of all learned abstracts that lie within our conscious and subconscious thoughts. To a degree, our "inheritance of knowledge" is acquired through a somewhat subtle, subliminal, filtering process, of sorts. Much of the knowledge revealed in this book, however, is specified in the bibliography, and most of this information clearly is in the public domain of coaches and fans, alike.

The following account may appear redundant, but the sources will explain, in part, the background from which the author's analogies for the evolution of I-formation football have emerged.

Ken Lyons

>Items listed in Chronological Order that relate to the Flexing Offense, either directly or by association<

TEXTBOOKS

>Related readings from Prentice-Hall, Inc., Englewood Cliffs, New Jersey<

1. Bryant Paul W. (Bear) 'Building a Championship Football Team' (1960)

2. Martin, Ben 'Ben Martin's Flexible-T offense' (1961)

3. Spilsbury, Max R. 'Slot-T Football' (1961)

4. Ecker, Tom and Paul Jones 'Championship Football by 12 Great Coaches' (1962)

5. Gamble, Harry 'The Pro-T Offense in High School Football' (1962)

6. Gaither, A.S. (Jake) 'The Split Line T offense' (1963)

7. Rice, Homer 'The Explosive Short T' (1963)

8. Royal, Darrell and Blackie Sherrod 'Darrell Royal Talks Football' (1963)

9. Teague, Fdward L. 'The Unbalanced Line Open End T Offense' (1964)

10. Walker, Robert (Bob) 'The Swing End Offense' (1964)

11. Reebenacker, Noel 'How to Develop a Successful High School Passing Attack' (1965)

<Related Readings from Parker Publishing Company, Inc., West Nyack, N.Y.>

1. Kramer, Roy F. 'The Complete Book of the I-Formation' (1966)

2. Swanson, Robert 'Football's Multiple Spread T Offense' (1966)

3. Coaching Clinic (Board of Editors) 'The Best of Football from the Coaching Clinic' (1967)

4. Dyer, Pete 'The Flip-Flop Offense in High School Football' (1967)

5. Graves, Ray 'Ray Graves' Guide to Modern Football Offense' (1967)

6. Kapral, LCDR. Frank S. 'Illustrated Guide to Championship Football' (1967)

7. Henry, Ed 'Developing a Successful High School Pro Set Football Offense' (1968)

8. Dooley, Vincent J (Vince) 'Developing a Superior Football Control Attack' (1969)

9. Harlow, Henry 'Winning Football with the Strategic Slot' (1969)

10. Stielstra, Jay 'Michigan Style High School Football' (1969)

11. Tallman, Drew 'Directory of Football Defenses: Success Defenses and How to Attack Them' (1969)

12. Andros, Dee G. and Rowland P. (Red) Smith 'Power T Football' (1971)

13. Tallman, Drew 'Winning Play Sequences in Modern Football' (1971)

14. Rice, Homer 'Homer Rice on Triple Option Football' (1973)

15. Ray, Gary F. 'Coach's Guide to the Slot I Offense' (1974)

16. Tallman, Drew 'Football Coach's Guide to a High Scoring Passing Offense' (1975)

17. Moglia, Joseph H. 'The Perimeter Attack Offense: Key to Winning Football' (1982)

18. Maddox, Jack 'Tight Slot Football: A Flexible Attack' (1983)

19. Bluth, Doug 'Football's Twin-I: A Complete Multiple Option Attack' (1984)

20. Smith, Homer 'Football Coach's Complete Offensive Playbook' (1987)

<Related Readings from Other Publications, as acknowledged>

1. Camerer, Dave 'Winning Football Plays by America's Foremost Coaches' The Ronald Press, New York, N.Y. (1962)

2. Edwards, Lavell and Normal Chow 'Winning Football with the Forward Pass' Allyn and Bacon, Inc., Boston-London-Sydney-Toronto (1985)

3. McKay, John H. 'Football Coaching' The Ronald Press, New York, N.Y. (1966)

4. Devine, Dan and Al Onofrio 'Missouri Power Football' Lucus Brothers Publishers, Columbia, Missouri (1967)

5. Hayes, Woodrow W. (Woody) 'Hot Line to Victory' Printed for author by Typographic Printing Co., Columbus. Ohio (1969)

6. Parseghian, Ara and Tom Pagna 'Parseghian and Notre Dame Football' Men-in-Motion, P.O. Bx 428, Notre Dame, Indiana (1971)

7. Holtz, Lou 'The Offensive Side of Lou Holtz' Lithographed for author by Parkin Printing Co., Little Rock, Ark(1978)

8. Wagner, Bob 'Getting the Edge: Hawaii Football' Mutual Publishing, Honolulu, Hawaii (1993)

MAGAZINES

<Related Readings from Coach & Athlete, Atlanta, Georgia>

1. Vann, Thad (Pie) 'The Mississippi Southern Multiple "T" Running Attack (Nov 1959)

2. Graves, Ray 'Florida's Outside Offense' (Oct 1963)

<Related Readings from Athletic Journal, Evanston, Illinois)

1. Bachman, Charles W. 'Your Offense Needs a Wingback' (May 1957)

2. Cates, Smoky 'The Scissor Series' (May 1957)

3. Smith, Homer 'The Fundamentals of Forward Passing' (Mar 1961)

4. Carlson, Ronald P. 'The Philosophy of the Belly Series' (May 1961)

5. McVay, John E. 'Multiple Blocking Schemes for High School and College (Sep 1963)

6. Kapral, Lieut. Frank 'The Passing Attack' (Sep 1963)

7. Rowen, Vic 'The Man-in-Motion as an Offensive Weapon' (Sep 1963)

8. Mazzaferro, Peter 'The Isolation Series' (Oct 1963)

9. Kapral, Lieut. Frank 'Organization of the Passing Game' Part 1 (Oct 1963), Part 2 (Nov 1963), Part 3 (Dec 1963), Part 4 (Jan 1964), Part 5 (Feb 1964), Part 6 (Mar 1964)

10. Kapral, Lieut. Frank 'Pass Receiving' (May 1964)

11. Rowen, Vic 'Developing Faking Ability in a Pass Receiver'(May 1965)

12. Rowen, Vic 'Improve the Receiver's Pass Catching Ability' (June 1965)

13. Rapp, Victor M. 'The Short Slot with a Split End' (Sep 1965)

14. Wallace, Jack 'Fan Pass Series from a Tight Slot Formation' (Sep 1965)

15. Nitchman, Nelson W. 'The Sweep Aspect' (Mar 1966)

16. Hopkins, Mark L. 'The Flip-Flop I' (May 1966)

17. Katchmer, Nelson A. 'Passing Array' (Jun 1966)

18. O'Neal, Bill 'The Belly Series from the I' (May 1968)

19. Pont, John, Jake Yan Schoyck and Bob Baker 'Indiana's Wide I' (Sep 1968)

20. Graves, Ray, and Fred Pancoast 'Florida's Flexible I' (Apr 1969)

21. Stoltz, Dennis E. 'Attacking the Notre Dame 4-4 Defense' (May 1969)

22. Blackman, Robert (Bob) 'Updating the V Formation' (Apr 1970)

23. Carnicella, Ron 'Flip Series from the Power-I' (Sep 1969)

24. Huber, William F. 'A New Eye on the Power-I' (Sep 1969)

25. Reaves, Rhod and Irvin Whitehead 'Supplementing the Bifocal Set with the I Formation' (Sep 1969)

26. Yovicsin, John M. 'Harvard Sweep Series' (Sep 1969)

27. Boyle, Chuck 'Time Pattern Passing' (Sep 1970)

28. Rowen, Vic 'Dropback Passing Technique' (Sep 1970)

29. Shaughnessy, Clark D. 'The Modern T Formation' <a reprint> (Sep 1970)

30. Spadafora, Joseph 'Cross-Buck to Victory' (Sep 1970)

31. Athletic Journal staff, with input from collegiate coaches. 'Football through the Years' (Mar 1971)

32. Devine, Dan and Bob Frala 'Missouri's Slot-I' (Apr 1971)

33. Watson, Michael J. 'Power Sweep Series from a Slot-T' (Sep 1971)

34. Dean, Jack W. 'Catching the Football' (Apr 1972)

35. McClendon, Charlie 'LSU's Goal Line Attack' (May 1972)

36. Marciniak, Ron 'The Fundamentals for Trapping and Pulling Linemen' (Apr 1973)

37. Olivadotti, Thomas R. 'Releases off the Line of Scrimmage' (Apr 1973)

38. Curtis, Richard 'Offensive Line Strategy for the Inside Trap' (Mar 1974)

39. Reaves, Rhod 'Complementing the Power-I Set' (Apr 1974)

40. Sullins, S.E. 'Attack the 4-4 with an L Formation' (Apr 1974)

41. Wright, Jim 'Wichita's Counter Option Series' (Sep 1974)

42. Dooley, Vince and George Haffner 'Georgia's Perimeter Attack' (Aug 1982)

43. Dixon, Pat 'Blocking Patterns' (Sep 1982)

44. Herrington, John 'Sprint-Out Passing Attack' (Sep 1982)

45. Brock, Jeff 'Using the Belly and Companion Plays to Attack the Weak Side' (Feb 1983)

46. Culver, Jerry 'Complementing the Inside Running Game' (Aug 1983)

47. Hannaman, Keith 'The Power I' (Aug 1983)

48. Koehler, Michael 'The Fine Art of Throwing' (Aug 1983)

49. Roebuck, Gary 'Triple Option from the Wing Slot Formation' (Aug 1983)

50. Luke, B.J. 'The Sprint Draw' (Apr 1984)

51. Dooley, Bill and Pat Watson 'The Virginia Tech Isolation Series' (Mar 1985)

52. Donahue, Terry and Homer Smith 'UCLA Runs to the Roses' (Apr 1986)

53. DeBerry, Fisher 'Passing from the Wishbone' (Aug 1986)

<Related Readings from Scholastic Coach, New York, N.Y.>

1. University of Missouri Coaching Staff 'Something Special (Missouri's Power Sweep)' (Oct 1962)

2. Thompson, Bill 'Southern Cal's Shifting T.' Part 1 (Sep 1963), Part 2 (Oct 1963), Part 3 (Nov 1963)

3. Barry, John M. 'Flexible Blocking Calls' <Box-T:V-Formation> (Jun 1971)

4. Rosato. Nick 'Triple Option Attack from I-Slot' (Sep 1971)

5. Ralston, Bob 'Blocking the Contain on Triple Option' (Apr 1972)

6. Adelphi University (NY) <Photo demostrations> 'Three Plays from Slot-I (Off-Tackle, Split Buck & Scissors)' (May 1972)

7. Haushalter, William J. 'Veer Series from the Tandem I' (May 1972)

8. Dinaberg, Bob 'Special Power-I Goal-Line Offense' (Jun 1972)

9. Gamble, Harry 'Shifting I and Triple Option' (Sep 1972)

10. Holtz, Lou 'Slant and Outside Veer from Twin Veer Offense' (Sep 1974)

11. Dooley, Bill 'North Carolina's Bread and Butter Sprint Draw' (May 1976)

12. Dunn, Mike 'Counter Option Series from the Basic Slot-I' (May 1976)

13. Laycock, Jimmye 'Attacking the Perimeter from the Clemson "I"' (May/Jun 1978)

14. Gallery, Jim 'Fullhouse Inside Belly' (May/June 1980)

15. Donahue, Terry 'UCLA's Basic 'I' Tailback Play and Complements' (May-Jun 1981)

16. Huey, Gene 'Nebraska's Sprint-Out Pass vs. All Coverages' (Sep 1982)

17. Starace, Rick and Joe Puggelli 'Seconding the "Motion" in the I Veer Option Offense' (May/Jun 1983)

18. Sprague, Dale L. 'Weakside Running Attack vs. the Loaded 50 Defense' (Aug 1983)

19. DeBerry, Fisher and staff 'Air Force Academy's Wishbone Triple Option Offense' (Aug 1986)

20. Capone, Skip 'Winning with a Two-Minute Drill' (Aug 1986)

21. Maloney, Richard 'How Penn Attacks & Controls the LOS with Zone Blocking' (Aug 1987)

22. Johnston, Lew 'Dictate the Defense with a T-Bone'(Aug 1987)

23. Tricaro, Joseph 'Stalk Blocking the Deep Inside Third' (Dec 1988)

24. Partridge, Jerry and Jay Partridge 'A Strongside Power/Sprint Draw Series' (Nov 1990)

25. O'Boyle, Mike 'Reading the Option from the Triple-I' (May/Jun 1991)

26. Barnett, Gary 'Colorado's I-Bone Offense' (Aug 1991)

27. Cherplick, Craig 'Building Line Play Through Fundamentals' (Oct 1991)

28. Wells, Lyle 'Get an Edge with an I-Bone' (Nov 1991)

29. Mountjoy, Bill & Bob Buck 'Attacking 3-Deep Zone Coverage' (Sep 1993)

30. Miran, Karl 'Perimeter Attack from an I Option Offense' (Oct 1994)

31. Knott, Chris L. 'Check and Checkmate: Forcing the Defense to Adjust with Unbalanced Sets'(May/June 1995)

BOOKLETS:

-Related readings from the American Football Coaches Association Proceedings and Summer Manuals. Administrative offices in Waco, Texas- (* indicates Proceedings from clinics: ** indicates Summer Manual presentations)

1. Smith, Larry, and Linde Infante 'Green Wave Passing Attack' *1980

2. English, Wally 'Pitt's Explosive Passing Attack' **1980

3. Fisher, Jack 'Powering our Way to a Championship' **1980

4. Kinnan, Joe 'Utilizing the Fullback in the I-Formation. **1980

5. McMillan, Terry 'Mississippi College's Strong-side Attack' **1980

6. Bowden, Bobby 'Florida State's Passing Principles' *1981

7. Jeffries, Willie, and Larry Beckish 'The Tight Option and Turnback Draw' *1981

8. Kidd, Roy "Eastern Kentucky's Running Game' *1981

9. Haushalter, William 'Navy's Ground Attack' **1981

10. Arban, J.C. 'Pearl River Passing Game' *1982

11. Collins, Bobby 'The Southern Mississippi Sprint-out Series *1982

12. Pate, Bobby, and Chuck Taylor West Georgia's Multiple-I National Championship Offense' *1983

13. Anderson, Dick 'Penn State's Outside Attack from the I-Formation' **1983

14. Sekul, George 'Quarterback Easy Read' **1983

15. Shoup, Robert F. 'A Safe and Sane Strategy for Third-and-Long Yardage' **1983

16. Foley, Mike 'Building a Running Game off Sprint Action' **1984

17. Edwards, LaVell 'BYU Pass Pattern Adjustments *1985

18. Coker, Larry 'Misdirection: A Must for Offensive Success' **1985

19. Corrao, Pete 'Keeping an "I" on the Goal Line' **1985

20. DeBerry, Fisher 'The Passing Game from the Wishbone' *1986

21. Teaff, Grant 'Moving the Chains with a Short-Yardage Offense' *1986

22. MacPherson, Dick 'The Syracuse Option Game' **1986

23. Jackson, Tom, Russ Burns, and Jim Hollis 'Variations off the Sprint Draw' **1987

24. DeLeone, George 'Placing the Defense in a Pass-Run Bind' **1988

25. Shealy, Dal 'Scoring Inside the Opponent's 20-yard Line with the I Formation' **1988

26. DiNardo, Gerry 'Scoring From Inside the 10-yard Line' **1989

27. DeBerry, Fisher 'What Makes Birds Fly' *1990

28. Whipple, Mark 'Offset the I For Leverage' **1990

29. Kinnan, Joe 'Manatee's Trap Option Offense' *1992

30. Sheridan, Dick 'Simple Adjustments and Coverages for the Complex Passing Game' *1992

31. Schmidt, Pete 'Albion's Methods of Modern Zone Blocking' **1992

32. Thomas, Roger 'Make Them Spin with the Sweep and Counter' **1992

33. Wallace, Bobby 'Championship Options from North Alabama's Slot-I' *1994

34. Schmidt, Pete 'The Albion Championship Offense' *1995

35. Osborne, Tom 'Nebraska's Offensive Variations' *1995

36. House, Jim 'Nevada's Inside Zone' **1995

37. Nielson, Bob 'The Wartburg Zone Running Game' **1995

38. Hollis, Joe, Walt Harris, Mike Jacobs, and Tim Spencer 'Ohio State's Record-Breaking Offense' *1996

39. Lee, David 'Rice's Mid-Line Option' **1998

-Related readings from the American Football Quarterly—An Insider's Perspective, American Football Quarterly Publishing Company, P.O. Box 1825, Manhatten, Kansas.

1. Turner, Ron 'Keep the Chains Moving' (Illinois 3rd Down Attack) Volume 4, 3rd Quarter, 1998.

<Mississippi Assn. of Coaches Clinic handouts>

1. Vann, Thad (Pie) 'Mississippi Southern's Offense' (Aug 1956)

2. Curtice, Jack 'Stanford's Passing Offense/Tactics' (Aug 1960)

3. Dobbs, Glenn 'Tulsa Passing Game' (Aug 1967)

4. McPhail, Hartwell and Leo Jones 'Integrating the Wing-T and I Formation' (Aug 1967)

5. Rutter, Hollis 'Belly Series with Pulling Guard' (Aug 1968)

6. Fairbanks, Chuck and Barry Switzer 'Oklahoma Slot-I' (Aug 1969)

<University of Arizona, 1984>

1. Bernardi, Gary 'TE Play and the Y Option Route' 'Pass Route Adjustments' 'Running Back Routes'

2. Blocking Fundamentals/Line calls and Tecniques

<18th Florida Annual Coaches Assn. Clinic, Gainsville, Fla, Aug. 1966>

1. Dickey, Doug 'Tennessee Offense'

2. Dunn, Jimmy 'Tennessee Running Offense & Play-Action Passes'

3. Pancoast, Fred 'The Gator Aerial Game'

4. Prater, Jack 'Miami Offensive Line Play'

<Georgia Athletic Coaches' Clinic Notes, Atlanta, Ga., 1966>

1. Dooley, Vince and staff 'Georgia Philosophy & Offense' <Wing-T>

<Holiday Clinic, Daytona Beach, Florida, Jan 1967>

1. Meyer, Ken 'Alabama's Passing Offense' <Pro T>

<Kodak Football Coach of the Year Clinic, Atlanta, Ga., Feb 1967>

1. Cahill, Tom ' West Point Offense'

2. Claiborne, Jerry 'Sprint Out Pass'

3. Daugherty, Duffy 'Spartan Offense'

4. Dooley, Vince 'Georgia's Offense'

5. Graves, Ray 'Florida Passing Game'

6. Owen, Tommy 'Montgomery Bell Offense'

7. Russell, Erk   'Georgia Line Play'

8. Williamson, Richard
   'Alabama End & Wide Receiver Play'

Louisiana Football Coaches Assn>

1. Roberson, Millard
   'Verticle-Stretch Principle at
   the Line of Scrimmage' (1990)
   <reproduction courtesy of writer>

Louisiana State University
Spring Football Clinics>

1. Stovall, Jerry and staff
   'Offensive Fundamentals' (1981)
   High School Seminars:
   'Veer Offense' (J.T. Curtis),
   'Veer Blocking' (Jerry Fremin),
   and 'I Offense' (Chuck Herrington).

2. Arnsparger, Bill and staff
   'Organization of Offense' (1984)
   High School Seminars: 'John Curtis
   Practice Organization, and Neville's
   'Multiple Attack'

3. Arnsbarger, Bill and staff
   'QB, RB, Receiver & Linemen Techniques and Drills' (1985)

<University of Louisville 1991>

1. Protection Schemes/Pass Patterns

<Utah State University 1980>

1. Shea, Terry
   'The Quarterback'

Scholastic Coach Football Clinic
Notes>   Volume 1

1. Corso, Lee "I Formation" <Stack I>

2. Crowder, Eddie 'Triple Option &
   Sprint Out' <Slot-I>

3. Devaney, Bob "Running from Slot-I'

4. Gamble, Harry "Triple Option
   from the I <Slot>

5. Majors, Johnny 'Option & Passing
   Game'

6. Schembechler, Bo   'Michigan Power
   Offense'

          Volume 2

. Bowden, Bobby   'The Play-Action
  Passing Game'

. Crowder, Eddie   "Planning the
  Option Series Offense'

. Farrell, Ed   'The Power
  Blast Offense'

4. Madden, John   'The Ball
   Control Passing Game'

5. MacPherson, Dick   'The Sprint-
   Out, Roll-Out Passing Game'

<Texas Coach by Texas High School
Coaches' Assn., Austin, Texas>

1. Parseghian, Ara 'Northwestern
   Isolation Series' (Sep 1960)

2. Schwartzwalder, Ben 'Demonstration:
   Line Blocking vs. Stunt Defense'
   (Sep 1960)

3. Devine, Dan   'Missouri Power
   Offense'   (Sep 1963)

4. Dotsch, Rollie   'Missouri
   Blocking Rules'   (Sep 1963)

5. North, John   'LSU's Offensive
   Ground Attack' + 'LSU's Offensive
   Line Blocking and Drills' (Sep 1964)

6. Barfield, Bob 'The Spread T
   Offense'   (Sep 1965)

7. Moore, Bob   'Drills to Develop the
   Offensive Linemen' + 'Offensive
   Line Play'   (Sep 1965)

8. Broyles, Frank   'The Pro "I"
   Offense at Arkansas' (Sep 1966)

9. Dooley, Vince 'Attacking
   the Corner'   (Sep 1968)

10. Coleman, Bob   'Jayton
    Tailback Series' (May 1969)

<College & University Playbooks:
Courtesy of Coaching Staffs>

1. Mississippi Southern College
   (University of Southern Mississippi)
   'Multiple T Offense' (1955)

2. University of Tennessee
   'Veer T & I Formation Offense'
   Extract for clinics (1978)
   —Courtesy of Coach Roger Cook—

3. University of Nebraska
   'Basic Slot I Attack'
   Extract for clinics (1981)

4. Millsaps College
   'Millsaps Multiple Offense' (1990)
   —Courtesy of Coach Tommy Ranager—

5. <High School> 'Viking Football
   Handbook' —Courtesy of Al Tregle—

<University Drill-Book Handouts>

1. Louisiana Tech (1979 Camp)

2. Northeast Louisiana University <1981>

3. Tulane University <mid 1980's>
   'Quarterback Manual' <1985>

4. University of Southern Miss. <1978>
   (Roland Dale, AD; Bobby Collins, HC)

5. University of Texas, El Paso <1991>
   'Offensive Line Drill Manual'

<Medalist Sports News, Mar 1976
(#1-2), Sep/Oct 1979 (#3-5)>

1. Dry, F.A. 'The Passing Game'

2. Pancoast, Fred 'Ball Control
   Passing'

3. Bruce, Earl   'Pass Protection'

4. Osborne, Tom 'Nebraska Running Game'

5. Young, Jim   'Purdue Passing Game'

<Inside Coaching by Converse,
Fall 1986>

1. Brown, Kenneth   'Attacking
   the Split-Four'

Subscription Publications

<The Coaching Clinic, Prentice-
Hall, Inc, Englewood Cliffs, N.J>

1. Howard, Frank   'Clemson's
   Sprint-Out Pass'<Slot-T> (Apr 1967)

2. Welborn, Richard
   'Attacking the Man-to-Man Defense
   from a Slot-I Formation' (Apr 1967)

3. Crowley, Marv   'Complete Passing
   Game from the I Formation'(May 1967)

4. Noxon, Bill   'A "T" Side Belly
   Series in Slot Formation' (Oct 1967)

5. Cure, Sid   'The Pro I
   with Extended Motion' (Nov 1967)

6. Unruh, Paul   'The Shifty
   Winged-I Ground Attack' (Jan 1968)

7. Kloppenburg, Don 'The Passing Part
   of a Balanced Attack' (Apr 1968)

8. Jones, Donald M.   'The Play-Action
   Pass:A Salvatiion'<Wing-T>(Sep 1968)

9. Sotir, Alex 'Adapting Wing-T Off-
   Tackle Series to the I' (Sep 1968)

10. Carnicella, Ron 'Complementing the
    Power I with Flip Series' (Oct 1968)

11. Dunn, Lawrence   'Running the Off-
    Tackle Play from the I' (Mar 1970)

<The Football Clinic, Parker Publishing Co, Inc, West Nyack, N.Y>

1. Cummings, R.E. 'Adapting the I Formation into your Offense' (Oct 1967)

2. Chai, Calvin 'The Quick Toss Series (Mar 1968)

3. Welborn, Richard E. 'Beating Man-to-Man Defenses with Strong-Side Pass Patterns'(Mar 1968)

4. King, J.T. 'Developing Pass Receivers' (Jun 1968)

5. Keller, Ollie 'Option Plays from two I-Formations' (Jun 1968)

MAIL-OUT PAMPHLETS

1. Berndt, Jerry and staff 'Pennsylvania Playbook: Counter Series' <University of Pennsylvania>

2. Blackman, Bob and staff 'Cornell "Read on the Run" Pass Scheme' <Cornell University>

3. Conover, Al 'Progression Drill' (blocking) <Rice University>

4. Crouthamel, Jake and staff 'Dartmouth College Counter Game' 'The Dartmouth Option Game' 'Dartmouth's Quick Passing Game' 'Dartmouth Screen Passes' <Dartmouth College>

5. Hallman, Curley (USM) 'Toss Sweep from I Formation' Chalk Talk, From The Sideline Institute For Wellness & Sports Medicine, Hattiesburg, Miss.

6. Schroeder, Tad and staff Short Yardage 'Inside Belly' 'Receiver Routes' U.S. Coast Guard Academy

7. Smith, Homer 'The Army Pass Receiving Game' The United States Military Academy

8. Tammariello, Augie 'Play Pulling' & 'Receiving and Net Drill Techniques' <University of Southwestern La.>

9. Young, Jim 'Toss Sweep'(application) Army Advisor <West Point, N.Y.>

10. Yukica, Joe 'Pass Offense Thoughts' 'The 1 Back Set' <Dartmouth College>

11. Quarterback & Receiver Camp Coaching Hints: Newsletter No. 1 'The Fade' Santa Barbara, Ca

Influencial CLINIC SPEAKERS (Offense) -(author's 35 years of exposure)-

<Gulf Coast Coaching Clinic: Lindy Callahan* & Leo Jones, sponsors>

(Collegiate)

Lynn Amedee (A & M Patterns), Mike Archer (organizational), (Bruce Ariens (MSU Passing Technique), Terry Bowden (Auburn I), Mack Brown (Tulane Trap Options), Watson Brown (MSU Options), Jim Carmody (USM program), Bobby Collins & Whitey Jordan (USM Option-I), Ernie Duplechin (McNeese Options), Rocky Felker (UA Patterns), Tom Goode (MSU themes), Walt Harris (UT Screens), Leo Jones (MSU Short Yardage), Tom Jones (Auburn Patterns), Wayne McDuffie (FSU), Al Onofrio (Missouri Power-I), Red Parker (UM Options), Homer Rice (UA Patterns), Jackie Sherrill (MSU Scoring Zone), Ron Tomain (TU Goal Line), Rick Trickett (MSU Schemes), Bob Tyler (UA/MSU Patterns), John Williams (MC program), Jim Wright (UT Option Schemes & Patterns).

(Junior College)

Ray Ishee and Bob Ricketts (Pass Protection), George Sekul (QB techniques).

(High School)

Doug Barfield (I Sets), Ozzie Blaize (Wing-T/I), Lindy Callahan (Organizational), Jim Crossland (Developmental), Pat Culpepper (Pro-I), Jesse Daigle (Patterns), Nick Hyder (Pro Sets), Tom Freeman (Veer-T), Charlie Hall (Power-I), Bert Jenkins (Pride Management), Mike Justice (Off-Set I), Doug Merchant (Organizational), Lewis Murray (Pro-I), John McKissick (Option Attack), Buddy Singleton (organizational), Dwight Thomas (Multiple Sets), Lum Wright (Organizational), Willis Wright (Trap Schemes).

*Note: Lindy Callahan & Roland Dale (USM) both were an educational influence to the author as his high school coaches and as college instructors for required accreditation courses in football.

<Houston Clinic>

Ben Martin (AFA Offense/program).

<Louisiana High School Coaches Association Clinics>

(Collegiate)

Mack Brown, Greg Davis, & Darrell Moody (Tulane Trap Option & Patterns), John David Crow (Foundational), Eddie Crowder (CU Slot-I), Lavell Edwards, Norman Chow & Roger French (BYU Pro-T), Lou Holtz & Larry Beightol (Twin-Veer), Frank Kush (ASU Trapping/Passing), Oscar Lofton (USL Patterns), Steve Sloan, Tom Goode, and Mike Pope (UM I & Veer Patterns), Larry Smith & Steve Axman (Arizona Multiple Sets), Grant Teaff (Baylor I).

(High School)

Lewis Cook (Sprint Patterns), Larry Dautrieve (Sprint Patterns), Jack Gray (Pro-T Patterns), Lee Hedges (Pro-I & T Patterns), Easton Roth (I Sets), Jack Salter (I Sets), Butch Stoker (Patterns).

<LSU CLINICS>

Paul Dietzel & Charlie McClendon with staff(s): Lynn Amedee, Jim Collier, Doug Hamley, Lynn LeBlanc, Dave McCarty, Charlie Pevey, Scooter Purvis, Craig Randall, Barry Wilson and Jerry Stovall. (Offensive Topics: LSU's Multiple-I + Drills & Program). Special Guest Speakers at LSU Clinic: Ralph Staub (OSU Slot-I), Darryl Rogers (Michigan State Patterns).

<Mississippi Association of Coaches and Mississippi Education Assn.>

(Collegiate)

Frank Broyles (Arkansas Slot-I), Jack Curtice (Stanford Patterns & Strategy), Keith Daniels (USM I/Veer), Frank Howard & Charley Waller (Clemson-T), John McKay (USC Shifty-I), Dick Sheridan & Ted Cain (NCS Tight Option), Steve Spurrier (QB Development), Grant Teaff (Baylor Power-I), Murray Warmath (Minnesota Patterns/Techniques), George Welsh (UV Pro-I).

(High School)

Bob Dunaway (Flanker T), Paul Pounds (Slot-I Options), Reese Snell (Unbalanced-T), Bob Tyler (Pro-T), Greg Wall (Flexbone Patterns), John Williams (Flanker-T).

<Nichols State Clinics>

Roland Acosta (Patterns), Rod Baker (Pro-I), Tommy Fernandez (Structural), Billy Miller (Pro-T), Butch Troy (Schemes).

<Southeastern Clinics>

Billy Brewer, Ken Magee & Bob Ricketts (SLU Wingbone), Whitey Jordon (USM Veer w/Blocking Techniques), Lewis Murray (Patterns), Otis Washington (Pro & Veer Sets).

<Tulane Clinics>

J. T. Curtis (Veer-T), Buddy Geis (TU Patterns), Vince Gipson (TU Organization), Oscar Lofton (TU Patterns), Ken Meyers (TU Offense), Frank Monica (I Patterns/TU attack), Darrell Moody (TU Options), Jack Salter (Organizational).

<USM Clinics>

Bobby Collins & Whitey Jordon (Veer-T/Pro-I Trap Options), Jeff Bower (Receivers), Jim Carmody (Organizational), Milo McCarthy (Running Backs).

<Millard Roberson Clinic>

Ken Lyons (Passing Techniques), in structured contrast with Chipper Simon (Wing-T Principles).

TO MY COACHING AFFILIATES WHO HAVE SHARED THEIR EXPERTISE AND KNOWLEDGE THROUGH CLINICAL AND PERSONAL DISCUSSIONS, THROUGH WRITINGS AND PERSONAL EXAMPLE, *I WISH TO EXPRESS MY GENUINE GRATITUDE.* I WISH, ALSO, TO EXPRESS MY APPRECIATION TO COLLEGIATE COACHES BOBBY COLLINS, WHITEY JORDAN, BOB RICKETTS, AND FRANK MONICA WHO, LIKE COUNTLESS OTHER COACHES, WERE ALWAYS HOSPITABLE AND LIKEWISE AVAILABLE TO TALK FOOTBALL AT GREAT LENGTHS. TO RICK TRICKETT AND RONNIE CUEVAS, MANY *THANKS* FOR YOUR INPUT INTO THE UPDATED BLOCKING TECHNIQUES.

Ken Lyons

INDEX

--BIBLIOGRAPHY excluded--